A VISITOR'S

THE BATTLES OF ARRAS
NORTH

Vimy Ridge to Oppy Wood
and Gavrelle

The ruins of Mont-St-Eloi Abbey.

A Visitor's Guide

The Battles of Arras North

Vimy Ridge to Oppy Wood and Gavrelle

Jon Cooksey
& Jerry Murland

Pen & Sword
MILITARY

An imprint of
Pen & Sword Books Ltd
Yorkshire – Philadelphia

First published in Great Britain in 2019 by
PEN & SWORD MILITARY
An imprint of
Pen & Sword Books Ltd
Yorkshire – Philadelphia

ISBN 978 1 47389 303 0

A CIP catalogue record for this book is available from the British
Library

Typeset in Ehrhardt by
Mac Style
Printed and bound in the UK by CPI Group (UK) Ltd,
Croydon, CRO 4YY

Pen & Sword Books Ltd incorporates the Imprints of Aviation,
Atlas, Family History, Fiction, Maritime, Military, Discovery,
Politics, History, Archaeology, Select, Wharncliffe Local History,
Wharncliffe True Crime, Military Classics, Wharncliffe Transport,
Leo Cooper, The Praetorian Press, Remember When, White Owl,
Seaforth Publishing and Frontline Publishing.

For a complete list of Pen & Sword titles please contact
PEN & SWORD BOOKS LTD
47 Church Street, Barnsley, South Yorkshire, S70 2AS, England
E-mail: enquiries@pen-and-sword.co.uk
Website: www.pen-and-sword.co.uk

Or

PEN & SWORD BOOKS
1950 Lawrence Rd, Havertown, PA 19083, USA
E-mail: Uspen-and-sword@casematepublishers.com
Website: www.penandswordbooks.com

CONTENTS

INTRODUCTION AND ACKNOWLEDGEMENTS

A Visitor's Guide, The Battles of Arras: North is the sixth in a series of guidebooks in which we have designed routes to provide the battlefield tourist with the opportunity to explore and appreciate the more remote parts of the Western Front. Most historians agree that Arras, and the almost continuous fighting that took place around it, made it one of the key battlegrounds on the Western Front, yet even after the centenary of the Battle of Arras, fought in April and May 1917, it still fails to attract the same volume of visitors which are drawn to Ypres to the north or the Somme to the south. To an extent this is understandable; the gradual residential, commercial and industrial development of Arras has inexorably encroached on

Ordnance found near Bullecourt in the summer of 2017 awaiting collection by the French Département du Déminage.

many of the battlefield sites that were once familiar to soldiers from both sides of the wire, yet, despite this, there is still a great deal to see in what was an absolutely vital sector of the Allied front.

Where possible we have used quiet roads and local pathways but please be aware that speeding traffic and farm machinery is always a possibility, even on the quietest of roads. Whilst we have ensured that vehicles are not left in isolated spots, we do recommend you take the usual precautions when leaving a vehicle unattended by placing valuables securely in the boot or out of sight, and, being northern France, it is always advisable to carry a set of waterproofs and have a sensible pair of boots or shoes to walk in. Within the built-up areas cafes and refreshment stops are usually open during normal hours but it is a good idea to take something to eat and drink when away from your vehicle for any length of time. Cyclists will recognize the need to use multi-terrain tyres on their bikes and require the use of a sturdier hybrid or off-road machine. Regular visitors to the battlefields will be familiar with the collections of old shells and other explosive material that is often placed by the roadside by farmers. By all means look and take photographs but please do not touch as much of it is still in an unstable condition.

The historical information provided with each route has of necessity been limited but we have given an overview around which to develop your understanding of what took place and why. Nevertheless, we have made some additional suggestions for further reading which should widen your appreciation of the events that took place on this sector of the Western Front over 100 years ago. Visitors to the German cemeteries at Neuville-St-Vaast and St-Laurent-Blangy will appreciate the section covering equivalent ranks, as will those visiting the French National Cemeteries at Notre-Dame de Lorette and La Targette. Those of you who wish to find the last resting place of the soldier poets and writers or the Victoria Cross winners will find the relevant section in the appendices of some use.

In acknowledging the help of others we must thank Sebastian Laudan for his wonderful assistance in researching German accounts of the battles, Paul Oldfield for his present day photograph of the battlefield north of Gavrelle, Peter Oldham for his advice on various pill-boxes in the area and Nigel Cave for his assistance with maps of the underground cavities that lie hidden beneath the Arras landscape.

VISITING MILITARY CEMETERIES

The concept of the **Imperial War Graves Commission (IWGC)** was created by **Major Fabian Ware** (1869–1949), the volunteer leader of a Red Cross mobile unit which saw service on the Western Front for most of the period of the war. Concern for the identification and burial of the dead led Ware to begin lobbying for an organization devoted to burial and maintenance of those who had been killed or died in the service of their country. On 21 May 1917 the Prince of Wales became the president of the IWGC with Fabian Ware as its vice-chairman. Forty-three years later the IWGC became the **Commonwealth War Graves**

Fabian Ware was the first vice-chairman of the IWGC.

Commission (CWGC). Neither a soldier nor a politician, Ware was later honoured with a knighthood and held the honorary rank of major general. The commission was responsible for introducing the standardized headstone which would bring equality in death regardless of rank, race or creed and it is this familiar white headstone that you will see now in CWGC cemeteries all over the world. CWGC cemeteries are usually well signposted with the familiar green and white direction indicators and where there is a CWGC plot within a communal cemetery, such as **Camblain l'Abbé Communal Cemetery**, the familiar

The headstone marking the grave of Private Charles Mossery at Bois-Carre British Cemetery is of a standard pattern which you will find on all First and Second World War graves. Post-war CWGC headstones have a notch in either shoulder.

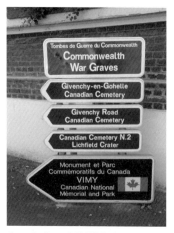

A profusion of CWGC signposts in Neuville-St-Vaast.

green and white sign at the entrance, with the words *Tombes de Guerre du Commonwealth* will indicate their presence. The tall Cross of Sacrifice with the bronze Crusader's sword can be found in many cemeteries, where there are relatively large numbers of dead. The larger cemeteries, such as **Cabaret Rouge British Cemetery**, also have the rectangular shaped Stone of Remembrance. A visitor's book and register of casualties is usually kept in a bronze box by the entrance. Sadly, a number of registers have been stolen and to prevent this from happening you may find a cemetery register in the local *Mairie*.

CWGC cemeteries are noted for their high standards of horticultural excellence and the image of rows of headstones set amidst grass pathways and flowering shrubs is one every battlefield visitor takes away with them. On each headstone is the badge of the regiment or corps or, in the case of Commonwealth forces, the national emblem. Below that is the name and rank of the individual and the date on which they died together with any decoration they may have received. Where the headstone marks the grave of a non-Christian, the emblem most commonly associated with their faith replaces the simple cross. Headstones of Victoria Cross winners have the additional motif of the decoration inscribed on it. At the base of the headstone is often an inscription chosen by the family.

Headstones marking the unidentified bear the inscriptions chosen by Rudyard Kipling, 'A Soldier of the Great War' or 'Known unto God'. Special memorials are erected to casualties known to be buried in the cemetery but whose precise location is uncertain.

CWGC burials in communal cemeteries are marked by a green and white sign containing the words Tombes de Guerre du Commonwealth *at the entrance.*

French War Graves

There are two French national cemeteries in the area covered by this guidebook, the *Nécropole Nationale de Notre-Dame de Lorette* and the *Nécropole Nationale*

Neuville-St-Vaast La Targette on the D938, but the visitor will find the concrete white grave markers used by the French *Ministère de la Défense et des Anciens Combattants* in a number of CWGC cemeteries and plots. French military cemeteries are usually marked by the French national flag and those which are contained within communal cemeteries are often indicated by a sign at the cemetery entrance bearing the words: *Carre Militaire, Tombes de Soldats, Morts pour la France.*

French war graves within communal cemeteries are marked with a distinctive blue and white sign at the entrance.

German Cemeteries
The German War Graves Commission – *Volksbund Deutsche Kriegsgräberfürsorge* – is responsible for the maintenance and upkeep of German war graves in Europe and North Africa. As with CWGC cemeteries, these are clearly signposted with a black and white sign bearing the words *Deutscher Soldatenfriedhof*. Visitors to the German cemetery south of Neuville-St-Vaast and that at St-Laurent-Blangy will find them both in stark contrast to CWGC cemeteries. They still exude a dark and often sombre ambiance exacerbated by the dark metal and stone grave markers bearing the name, rank, date of death and occasionally the unit. Like many French cemeteries, they contain mass graves for the unidentified and headstones with up to three or four names on each one.

German cemeteries are signposted with a black and white sign bearing the words Deutscher Soldatenfriedhof.

Equivalent Ranks
We have produced a rough guide to equivalent ranks which should assist you when visiting the cemeteries and memorials referred to in the guidebook.

British	German	French
Field Marshal	Generalfeldmarschall	Maréchal de France
General	Generaloberst	Général d'Armée
Lieutenant General	General der Infanterie/Artillerie Kavallerie	Général de Corps Armée
Major General	Generalmajor	Général de Division
Brigadier General	No equivalent rank	Général de Brigade
Colonel	Oberst	Colonel
Lieutenant Colonel	Oberstleutnant	Lieutenant Colonel
Major	Major	Commandant/Major
Captain	Hauptmann/Rittmeister	Capitaine
Lieutenant	Oberleutnant	Lieutenant
Second Lieutenant	Leutnant	Sous Lieutenant
Warrant Officer	Feldwebelleutnant	Adjutant
Sergeant Major	Offizierstellvertreter	Sergent Major
Sergeant	Vize-Feldwebel	Sergent
Corporal	Unteroffizer/Oberjäger	Caporal
Lance Corporal	Gefreiter/Obergefreiter	No equivalent rank
Private, Trooper, Sapper	Schütze/Grenadier/Jäger/ Musketier/Infanterist/Garde/ Soldat/Pionier/Fahrer/Füsilier Kanonier/Dragoner/Husar/ Kürassier/Ulan	Soldat/ Chasseur/ Artilleur/ Légionnaire

HISTORICAL CONTEXT

By 9 October 1914 the French Tenth Army, under the command of Général Louis Maud'huy, had managed to prevent a German occupation of Arras. To the north, the French had been pushed west from the Douai Plain, up and over the Vimy Ridge and off the heights of the Notre-Dame de Lorette spur. Neither side appeared to have the resources to encircle the other and, as the so-called 'race to the sea' ran off north and into Belgium, German attentions focussed on Ypres and the Yser and all hopes of a Christmas victory for the *Kaiser* were dashed by the spirited Belgian defence of the flooded land north of Ypres. The desperate fighting around that city itself in October and early November 1914 finally ended any hope of a 1914 German breakthrough to the Channel ports.

Général Louis Maud'huy in conversation with two of his men.

The First Battle of Artois (17 December 1914–13 January 1915)

With the French commander-in-chief, Général Joseph Joffre, as the plan's architect, Général Paul Maistre's XXI Corps attacked the northern and western outskirts of Carency in an attempt to seize the heights of Notre-Dame de Lorette. Simultaneous attacks by Général Hénri-Phillipe Petain's XXXIII Corps were pitted against the Berthonval Ridge and the north eastern outskirts of Arras by Général Gilbert Desforges' X Corps. It was a disastrous failure, with the French reporting casualties of some 30,000 killed, wounded and missing. In April 1915

Général Joseph Joffre was the French commander-in-chief until December 1916.

Général Victor d'Urbal replaced Général Louis de Maud'huy as commander of the Tenth Army.

The Second Battle of Artois, 9 May–18 June 1915

Carried out with British co-operation further north at **Aubers Ridge**, the initial French attack ruptured the German line and captured Vimy Ridge but reserve units were not able to reinforce the troops before German counter-attacks forced the French back, about half-way to their original jumping-off point. The British attack at Aubers Ridge (9 May 1915) was another costly failure and further offensive action was suspended until 15 May. Despite the setbacks, however, the French offensive had advanced the front line towards Vimy Ridge and established a significant foothold on the Notre-Dame de Lorette plateau. (The 1915 British battles, including the Battle of Loos, are covered in our visitor's guide to *The Battles of French Flanders*). On 12 May 1915 Carency was taken and Ablain-St-Nazaire fell soon afterwards. Neuville-St-Vaast was captured on 9 June and the German-held 'Labyrinth' trench complex fell eight days later. However, the cost in French casualties alone has been estimated at over 100,000, a figure that becomes even more staggering if the 27,684 British casualties are added.

The Third Battle of Artois, 25 September–11 October 1915

This offensive was conceived on the premise that the Allies would deliver simultaneous blows against the shoulders of the German-held Noyon Salient; the French hitting the Champagne sector and the Notre-Dame de Lorette spur with the British striking further north at Loos. The French XXXIII Corps took the Château de Carleul and Souchez and cleared the eastern slopes of Notre-Dame de Lorette; the crest of Vimy Ridge was again reached with French units reporting they were amongst the orchards of La Folie Farm. Once again the attack stalled in the face of powerful German counter-attacks and the French suffered another 50,000 casualties. **Loos**, the third British failure of the year, concluded with 50,000 casualties and the resignation of the British commander-

Sir Douglas Haig.

in-chief, **Sir John French**, who was replaced by **Sir Douglas Haig**. A number of historians have written off the Artois offensives as an expensive French bloodletting that achieved little but, in the authors' opinion, the continual French attacks in Artois not only squeezed the Germans into a tighter perimeter on Vimy Ridge, but facilitated the Canadian Corps' success in April 1917.

On 1 March 1916 the British XVII Corps, commanded by **Lieutenant General Sir Julian Byng**, took over the Vimy Sector and **Lieutenant General Sir Edmund Allenby's** Third Army began moving into position along the line east of Arras, facilitating the French Tenth Army's move to Verdun. The British occupancy of the Vimy Ridge sector was characterized by almost continuous mining operations that turned the front line into a maze of mine craters and resulted in the German attack of 21 May 1916 which drove the British 47th Division off the crest of the ridge and back towards Zouave Valley. A British counter-attack was prevented by Haig, who, at that time, was more than preoccupied with planning for the British offensive on the Somme which began on 1 July 1916. Three months later the Canadian Corps, now under the command of Julian Byng, was assigned to the Vimy Sector.

In December 1916, Joffre was replaced as French commander-in-chief by **Général Robert Nivelle**, who promised a new combined Allied offensive on the Aisne and at Arras. Charmed by Nivelle's rhetoric, **David Lloyd George**, the British Prime Minister, made little secret of his support for Nivelle and his distaste for the conduct of British operations on the

Lieutenant General Sir Julian Byng.

Lieutenant General Sir Edmund Allenby.

Robert Nivelle, the architect of the 1917 offensive.

Western Front. Thus, by the spring of 1917 Arras had become the focus of the next major British offensive albeit with the British playing a supporting role to the main French assault on the Aisne.

The Hindenburg Line

In late 1916, Royal Flying Corps (RFC) aviators reported the construction of a new double-trench system being dug some distance behind the existing front line. Running from Arras to Soissons in the south, it was known as the *Siegfried Stellung* by the Germans and the Hindenburg Line by the British, and would shorten the German front line by some 40km. From Tilloy-lès-Mofflaines the Hindenburg Line ran southeast behind Neuville Vitasse and down into the valley of the River Cojeul, before crossing the river between St-Martin-sur-Cojeul and Héninel and climbing Henin Hill. Curving to the east, it continued towards Fontaine-lès-Croiselles, dipping into the Sensée Valley to the west of Fontaine before ascending once again, this time onto the high ground known as 'The Hump', before it enveloped Bullecourt.

The order to retire behind the Hindenburg Line – codenamed *Alberich*, after the dwarf in Wagner's series of epic musical dramas *The Nibelung Ring Cycle* – was given on 4 February 1917. *Alberich* was to be preceded by five weeks of total devastation of the area to be evacuated; a scorched earth policy designed to deny the British the use of buildings or land and although it was not applauded by all German commanders, it allowed the Germans to withdraw effectively under the very noses of their enemy. The German retreat to the Hindenburg Line is officially recognized as occurring between 14 March and 5 April 1917, during which time there were a number of British actions against German outpost garrisons at Écoust-St-Mein, Croiselles and Hénin-sur-Cojeul. The British attack by the Third Army at Arras was confined to the northern sector of the Hindenburg Line where the zones of defence were still relatively incomplete, but further south they presented an altogether more difficult proposition.

The Arras Offensive, 9–14 April 1917

Due to the scope of this guide we have not been able to describe the subsidiary attacks on Fresnoy and Arleux-en-Gohelle. The opening attacks of the Arras Offensive can be divided into two battles; **Lieutenant General Sir Henry Horne's** First Army assault on Vimy Ridge and the **First Battle of the Scarpe**, involving Lieutenant General Edmund Allenby's Third Army, in which the First Army took Vimy

Ridge and the Third Army took most of their objectives including Monchy-le-Preux and the Wancourt Ridge; the area covered in more detail in the companion volume to this guide, *The Battles of Arras – South: Bullecourt, Monchy-le-Preux and the Valley of the Scarpe.*

Battle of Vimy Ridge, 9–14 April 1917	
I Corps: Lieutenant General Arthur Holland	24th Division
Canadian Corps: Lieutenant General Sir Julian Byng	1st–5th Canadian Infantry Divisions

First Battle of the Scarpe, 9–14 April 1917	
XVII Corps: Lieutenant General Sir Charles Fergusson	4th, 9th, 34th and 51st Divisions
VI Corps: Lieutenant General Sir Aylmer Haldane	3rd, 12th, 15th, 17th, 29th and 37th Divisions
VII Corps: Lieutenant General Thomas D'Oyly Snow	14th, 21st, 30th, 50th and 56th Divisions
Cavalry Corps: Lieutenant General Sir Charles Kavanagh	1st–3rd Cavalry Divisions

On 16 April Nivelle launched the **Second Battle of the Aisne** along the Chemin des Dames which was intended to break through the German lines and link up with the British in the north. It failed miserably and completely altered the rationale of the Arras offensive, forcing Haig to refocus his thinking. Thus, the **Second Battle of the Scarpe** was fought between 23 and 24 April, involving one division from the First Army and ten from the Third Army. Apart from the 63rd (Royal Naval) Division (RND)

Lieutenant General Sir Henry Horne.

taking Gavrelle in the First Army Sector, the largely under-strength Third Army made little progress, despite the 15th Division taking Guémappe.

Bullecourt

Again covered in more detail in the companion volume *The Battles of Arras – South: Bullecourt, Monchy-le-Preux and the Valley of the Scarpe* but included here to enhance the historical overview, the two attacks on Bullecourt were the preserve of Sir Hubert Gough's Fifth Army and the 1st ANZAC Corps. The first attempt was a total failure but the second managed to breach the Hindenburg Line and take the village.

Lieutenant General William Birdwood.

First Attack on Bullecourt, 11 April 1917	
V Corps: Lieutenant General Sir Edward Fanshawe	62nd (West Riding) Division
1 ANZAC Corps: Lieutenant General William Birdwood	4th Australian Division
Second Attack on Bullecourt, 3–17 May 1917	
V Corps: Lieutenant General Sir Edward Fanshawe	7th, 58th and 62nd Divisions
1 ANZAC Corps: Lieutenant General William Birdwood	1st, 2nd and 5th Australian Divisions

The Third Battle of the Scarpe

The battle began on 3 May and involved fourteen divisions along a 26km front and was designed to coincide with the second attack on Bullecourt. Unable to advance in the face of German resistance, the ill-fated and mostly unnecessary offensive was called off the next day. The Battle of Arras officially ended on 17 May, although a limited attack at Roeux on 5 June regained the remaining ground lost on 15/16 May, and it was here that the line stabilized for the remainder of 1917.

The German Spring Offensive, 1918

On 21 March 1918 Operation *Michael* was launched from the Hindenburg Line in the vicinity of St Quentin with the objective of breaking the Allied line. In the face of overwhelming German forces the British Fifth Army fell back in disarray. Much of the ground fought over was the residual wilderness of the Somme offensive of

1916 and was named the **First Battle of the Somme 1918** by the British Battles Nomenclature Committee, the French preferring to call it the **Second Battle of Picardy**. On 28 March 1918 the focus of the German attack switched to the British Third Army around Arras. Operation *Mars* was intended to breach the British defences north and south of the Scarpe, take Arras and secure the high ground of Vimy Ridge but, by this stage, the men on the ground knew what to expect and the German Seventeenth Army floundered against strong, well-organized defensive positions. By 5.00pm the offensive had ground to a halt on both sides of the Scarpe, with appalling German casualties. Nowhere had the German spearhead penetrated more than 2 miles and Arras remained firmly in British and Commonwealth hands leaving the Germans with few territorial gains.

The Advance to Victory
On 26 August the British First Army widened the attack on the Germans with the **Second Battle of Arras 1918**, which included the Battle of the Scarpe 1918 and the Battle of the Drocourt–Quéant Line (the German *Wotan Stellung*) on 2 September. The war had finally left Arras and the surrounding area behind as it moved east.

VISITING THE AREA

Visitors to the area can either stay in Arras or take advantage of the profusion of bed and breakfast and self-catering establishments in the area. If you are intending to base yourself in Arras the four-star **Hotel Mercure** near the railway station, which is situated on the Boulevard Carnot, offers the advantage of an underground car park. There are numerous other hotels in the city. The **Holiday Inn Express** on the Rue du Dr Brassart is also near the railway station whilst the three-star **Hotel Ibis Arras Centre les Places** is in the heart of the city on the Rue de Justice. A little further out the **Ace Hotel** on the D60 at Beaurains is located near Telegraph Hill and offers good, no-frills value with a restaurant/grill a short walk away. For those of you who wish for a more outdoor experience Camping la Paille Haute, at Boiry Notre Dame, is just over 6 miles from Arras and offers mobile homes to rent and has a heated swimming pool.

Using this Guidebook

The Arras area is characterized by its rolling hills and valleys and whilst walkers should have little difficulty, bikers will need a decent hybrid or off-road machine equipped with suitable tyres as some of the tracks we describe can become muddy after periods of wet weather. In compiling the guide we have taken the liberty of using a number of abbreviations in the text. With German units we have simply trimmed Infantry Regiment and Reserve Infantry Regiment to IR and RIR. Thus Infantry Regiment No. 73 becomes IR 73, Reserve Infantry Regiment No. 165 becomes RIR 165 and Fusilier-Regiment 90 becomes FR 90. British battalions and units have also been abbreviated, for example, the 4th Battalion Bedfordshire Regiment becoming 4/Bedfords. Where we refer to casualties the number quoted is usually taken from the battalion's war diary and includes officers and men who were killed, wounded or missing after the engagement.

Route Number	Route	Distance	🚶	🚲	🚗
1	Northern Car Tour	56km/35 miles		✔	✔
2	Vimy Ridge	12.2km/7.6 miles	✔	✔	
3	Villers-au-Bois	9.1km/5.6 miles	✔	✔	
4	Oppy Wood	2km/1.2 miles	✔	✔	
5	Gavrelle	11.9km/7.4 miles	✔	✔	
6	Arras Central – variable distance depending on the sites visited		✔	✔	✔

To assist you in your choice of route we have provided a summary of all six routes in the guidebook together with an indication as to their suitability for walkers, cyclists or car tourists. Distances are in km – the first figure in the table – and miles and to assist you in finding the starting point for each route we have provided the co-ordinates. The circular alpha/numeric references in the text of each route correspond directly with those on the relevant map. We hope you enjoy exploring the Arras battlefields as much as we have.

Route I

Northern Car Tour

A circular tour beginning at: Écoivres

Coordinates: 50°20′34.42″ N – 2°40′53.59″ E
Distance: 56km/35 miles
Suitable for: 🚗
Maps: IGN Série Bleue 2406O – Avesnes-le-Comte and 2406E – Arras

General description and context: We begin at the church on the D49, Rue Jean Baptiste Oboeuf, in Écoivres near Mont-St-Eloi, and conclude at the Bailleul Road West Cemetery, St-Laurent-Blangy, on the outskirts of Arras. The tour takes in the area to the west of the D937 Arras–Ablain-St-Nazaire road and looks at the fighting conducted by the French during the three Battles of Artois in addition to exploring the rear areas around Mont-St-Eloi, Camblain l'Abbé and Carency. We also visit Ablain-St-Nazaire before climbing the steep southern side of the Notre-Dame de Lorette spur to visit the French National Cemetery. Descending into Souchez, we drive south along the D937, stopping at the various memorials and cemeteries en route. After visiting the German cemetery, we turn north to Neuville-St-Vaast and the Canadian Memorial Park on Vimy Ridge before looking in detail at the actions that took place near the Claude, Cuthbert and Clarence mine craters near Bailleul Road West Cemetery.

Grafitti on the walls of the church at Écoivres.

Directions to start: Écoivres is best approached from the D341 which runs between Arras and Camblain l'Abbé.

Route description: The tour begins at the church at Écoivres where there is plenty of parking. Walk round the left side of the church and carved into the chalk stone of the walls at the far end you will find graffiti left by Canadians soldiers. Behind the church was the site of **Erie Camp**, whilst the building screened by the high wall you can see to the right of the church housed the 1st Canadian Division Headquarters. Being in the relatively safe rear area, Écoivres soon became host to two 'villages' of Nissen huts where battalions were withdrawn for rest and recuperation. The village school was used as a main dressing station, drawing many of its casualties from the advanced dressing station (ADS) at Aux Reitz. **Lieutenant Colonel Edward Hermon**, commanding 24/Northumberland Fusiliers, described his accommodation on 21 March 1917:

> Our huts are called Nissan [*sic*] and are like this: they are made of tin and lined with matchboard and they put them up in a couple of hours, almost. They are about 30ft long by 15ft wide and really very cosy and warm … One end is the pantry then a couple of blankets hung on a wire makes the dining room door and wall. At the other end we have six bunks, really quite comfortable.

From the church, continue through the village on the D49 until you see the war memorial where a CWGC signpost directs you to Écoivres Military Cemetery. Drive on past the communal cemetery to find the entrance to the cemetery on your right. There is room to park two cars on the side of the road directly in front of the cemetery and further parking is available at the communal cemetery.

Écoivres Military Cemetery
This cemetery is really the extension of the communal cemetery where the French had buried over 1,000 men from the Artois campaigns. The 46th (North Midland) Division took over the extension in March 1916, and their graves are in Plot I, Rows A to F. Successive divisions used the French military tramway to bring their dead in from the front-line trenches and, from the first row to the last, burials were made almost exactly in the order of date of death. You will find casualties from the British 25th Division attack on Vimy Ridge in May 1916 in Plots I and II and the 47th (London) Division burials from July and October 1916 in Plot III, Rows A–H. Plots V and VI contain the Canadian graves of men killed during the capture of Vimy Ridge in April 1917. Today the cemetery contains

Écoivres Military Cemetery.

1,728 Commonwealth burials, 13 of which are unidentified, together with 786 French and 4 German war graves.

This is a cemetery where, if you have not come here with any specific purpose in mind, it is possible to become overwhelmed amidst the headstones. With that end in mind we have highlighted nine casualties for you to visit; the first being **Lance Corporal James Holland** (II.E.17) of 10/Cheshires, who was executed on 30 May 1916. With the mysterious appearance of two suspected Germans who, just as mysteriously, disappeared, Holland falsely declared his post had been overrun and quit it with three of the men in his charge. The subsequent inquiry found this to be incorrect and he was convicted of cowardice. **Private Eugene Perry** (VI.C.7), aged 21 and serving with 22/Battalion – the French Canadian 'Van Doos', was another youngster shot by firing squad for deserting his post on 11 April 1917. He was one of twenty-five Canadians shot during the war – five of them in 22/Battalion. Perry had a reasonable record – apart from two brief absences – and on the second occasion had been absent for a little under 7 hours. But the Van Doos were seen as 'windy' and undisciplined after the Somme and Perry paid the price in CO Lieutenant Colonel Thomas Tremblay's crusade to restore his battalion's reputation and 'stiffen' its will.

Lieutenant Kenneth Campbell (IV.B.19) from the Canadian 42/Battalion was described by William Bird in his book *Ghosts have*

Warm Hands as rather naive and inexperienced. This was certainly the cause of his death on 23 January 1917 when he insisted on looking over the edge of **Vernon Crater** on Vimy Ridge. His brother, Lieutenant Colin Campbell, was killed in October 1917 serving with the Royal Field Artillery (RFA). **Driver Albert Morrison** (V.K.11), aged 22 and serving with the Canadian Field Artillery, had already been notified of his father's death, as a passenger on the SS *Lusitania*, when it was sunk on 7 May 1915. Albert was killed eighteen months later on 5 July 1917. Finally, **Lieutenant Colonel Michael Frederick Dennis** (V.L.1) took command of 7/8 KOSB on 27 May 1917 after relieving Lieutenant Colonel Sellar. His death by shellfire on 19 May 1918 left the battalion without their 'splendid and gallant' commanding officer. His funeral at Écoivres took place on 20 May. Four officers from 11/Lancashire Fusiliers (see **Route 2**) were killed on 15 May 1916 during the 74 Brigade attack on the **Crosbie Craters**. **Second Lieutenant Arthur McFarlan** (I.M.26) was killed by Crater Z whilst **Second Lieutenants William Barker** (I.N.12) and **Reginald Barrett** (I.N.15) were killed nearby at Craters V and W. The last of these men, **Second Lieutenant Edward Jewell** (I.M.11), died of his wounds the next day.

From the cemetery drive straight ahead for 600m until you reach a junction. Turn left and in a little under 1km you will reach the junction with the D341. Turn left here, passing over a crossroads to find the next turning on the right. This road leads uphill to Mont-St-Eloi.

Just before the abbey ruins a narrow footpath can be seen on the right which leads to the communal cemetery. You will also notice the entrance to the footpath has a CWGC signpost and another which directs you to the French 4th Dragoons Monument. Continue past the footpath and, after parking your vehicle opposite the abbey, walk back downhill to the pathway to visit the cemetery.

Mont-St-Eloi Communal Cemetery

During the war there were, apart from Écoivres Military Cemetery, two other cemeteries within the boundaries of the commune. Bray Military Cemetery and Mont-St-Eloi Military Cemetery were used extensively by both the French and British before the burials were moved after the Armistice to Écoivres and Cabaret Rouge British Cemeteries. Today, all that remains in the village is the communal cemetery where there are five headstones of British soldiers, all

The ruins of Mont-St-Eloi Abbey overshadow the communal cemetery.

killed on 22 May 1940 during a 'blue on blue' incident when French tanks returned the fire of two British anti-tank gun crews which had mistaken them for German tanks near Berthonval Farm. Sadly, one man remains unidentified. Erected in one corner of the cemetery is the **4e Régiment de Dragons Portés** (motorized infantry) Monument, which commemorates the fifty-seven officers and men of the regiment killed in the struggle against German panzers for Mont-St-Eloi in May 1940. The French graves are of those men who died in the fighting.

Mont-St-Eloi Abbey
Founded in the seventh century, the ruins of the abbey church you see today, and which can be accessed from the cemetery, date from the eighteenth century. Partly demolished after the French Revolution, it was severely damaged by German artillery in 1915 when it was believed the two towers were being used as observation points by the French during their attacks on Neuville-St-Vaast and Givenchy. The facade you see today is all that is left of the two towers. Thousands

of men were billeted here with the perhaps inevitable consequence of a pitched battle between the men of the 51st Highland Division and the Canadians prior to the assault on Vimy Ridge in April 1917. Whether this was the usual bad feeling over the different rates of pay between the British soldiers and their dominion cousins is anyone's guess, but such encounters were not uncommon. From the high ground of Mont-St-Eloi, Berthonval Farm can be made out if you look towards Vimy Ridge and the Canadian Monument, the farm buildings are screened by trees and situated 600m north of the D49; **Lieutenant General Julian Byng** used the farm as his advanced Corps Headquarters on 9 April 1917. Beyond the farm is Bois l'Abbe, where the French **Morrocan Division** assembled in May 1915 before its advance up to Thélus Mill and Vimy Ridge. On the flat ground to the southeast, south of Ste Anne Farm, **No. 8 Naval Air Squadron** of the Royal Naval Air Service (RNAS) – known as 'Naval Eight' – was in residence from May 1917 and many of the naval air aces flew from the aerodrome. It is said that **Major Chris Draper**, who commanded the squadron in 1918, performed a remarkable stunt by flying a Sopwith Camel between the two towers of the ruined abbey. Whether this feat is based on fact or was the result of an oft-spun and embroidered yarn remains unclear, but Draper was undoubtedly a skilful aviator. It is a fact that he flew an Auster under fifteen bridges along the River Thames in 1953!

Before you leave the abbey take a moment to call at the visitor's centre where you can obtain information regarding the extent of the former abbey buildings and a little of its varied history.

From Mont-St-Eloi retrace your route back to the D341 and turn right towards Camblain l'Abbé. Just before you enter the village, the large wood on the right – le Dessous de Perroy – was where the Canadian Artillery Camp was situated.

As you enter the village you will pass two large buildings on your right surrounded by a high wall with a set of large imposing gates in the centre. This is the unfinished chateau that was begun in 1820 by the wealthy Mathieu family but left uncompleted after family disputes provoked financial difficulties. What you see today are the buildings that were to form the two wings, the main part of the chateau never finished. During the early part of the war the chateau was occupied by the French, making way in 1916 for **Lieutenant General Byng**, who had his headquarters here. The village itself had

Lieutenant General Sir Julian Byng's HQ was in the unfinished chateau at Camblain l'Abbé.

developed into a mass of hutted encampments as **Lance Sergeant Frank Watts**, serving with 15/Battalion, The London Regiment (Civil Service Rifles), recalled on Sunday 21 May 1916:

> The battalion was in camp at Camblain l'Abbé, behind Vimy Ridge. Recent spells in the line had been quiet, the weather was warm and sunny, and everyone was in good spirits. I was on camp-cleaning fatigue, but, the camp being in a good condition, there was nothing to do beyond picking up an odd piece of paper or two. After dinner most of the men settled down in the hut to sleep or write letters; it was all very pleasant and happy, something like Sunday at home.

Park near the gates of the chateau and walk along the road for a few metres to a narrow tarmac path on the left – opposite the northern wing of the chateau – which leads up to the communal cemetery. Follow the path uphill for some 150m to reach the cemetery and, a little further on, the church via the Rue de l'Église. Notice the impact marks on the exterior of the church. Walk right around to the back of the church and note the graffiti carved into the walls by Canadian soldiers. Locate the name 'J W

Small'. This was carved by 39-year-old Private Joseph William Small who was born in Swanbourne, Buckinghamshire on 2 June 1879 but who had emigrated to Autoroad – now called Leacross – in Saskatchewan to farm the prairies. Small originally enlisted in the 188th (Saskatchewan) Battalion at Tisdale – also carved into the stone – on 27 March 1916 but was transferred to the 28th (Northwest) Battalion which had also recruited in Saskatchewan. The 28th spent several periods in divisional reserve in Camblain l'Abbe, the last of which was in late October 1917 before it moved north to take part in the last gasp of the Third Battle of Ypres on the Passchendaele Ridge. Did Joseph Small, a man born in Britain but obviously proud of his adopted country, carve his name at that time? Joseph Small was wounded during the successful attack which captured Passchendaele village, was evacuated but died on 8 November 1917. He is buried in Nine Elms British Cemetery west of Poperinge (VIII.C.11) but his name also survives here, a lasting legacy of his time spent on the Arras front.

Retrace your route to the village cemetery.

Camblain l'Abbé Communal Cemetery
This is a typical French communal cemetery containing a mixture of casualties from both world wars. There are several French graves along the northeastern boundary of the cemetery together with a single grave of an unknown German soldier, marked by a simple black metal cross. Individual German graves from the First World War are not unknown but are still relatively rare in French communal cemeteries and its location was revealed when it was pointed out to us by an elderly local resident. Three 1940 casualties from 12/Lancers are buried together at the far end of the plot.

Return to your vehicle and continue through the village towards Maisnil on the D341. In a little over 1km, just before the main road begins to rise, turn right for 200m along an unmarked road to reach the main road – marked Chaussée Brunehaut – on IGN maps. This is the Roman road that runs from Arras, northwest through Ferfay towards Thérouanne. Turn left here then bear right almost immediately at the fork to take a narrow road that leads uphill towards an obvious transmitter mast. After you enter the village take the first road on your right – Hameau du Maisnil – which takes you downhill to a crossroads. Turn left here and after 200m you will come to a pill-box in the field on your left.

The Maisnil Blockhouse

This machine-gun pill-box formed part of the GHQ Line that was constructed in anticipation of the 1918 German offensive and was to be the last line of defence before a retreat to the Channel ports became inevitable. That 'doomsday' option never came to pass but the pill-box is a tangible reminder of the seriousness with which the 1918 German offensives were viewed. You will already have passed another of these pill-boxes in the fields to the left of the road to Hameau du Maisnil as you headed downhill out of Maisnil towards the crossroads. The pill-box you are looking at now is one of six that remain from a network of defences that ran from Frévin-Capelle to the south, through Maisnil and north to Gouy-Servins and Bouvigny-Boyeffles. Built to a standard GHQ pattern with modifications, the squared lower exterior walls and rounded upper section is due to the method of construction rather than design considerations. In 1918 it would have been covered with earth and camouflaged with netting to avoid aerial observation.

Retrace your route to the crossroads and drive on, straight ahead – signposted D65 Villers-au-Bois and Carency. After 1.2km you will arrive at the twin pillars and gatehouse of the Château de la Haie. This is as far as you can go as the house and grounds are private property. However, a glance up the driveway will reveal what are probably the original cobbles laid when the chateau was built in the eighteenth century.

The Maisnil blockhouse was part of the GHQ Line.

Château de la Haie

Before the war the building was home to the actress Sarah Bernhardt but was burnt down in the 1950s, and a large house now stands in its place in the former chateau grounds. During the three Battles of Artois the chateau hosted the staff of French Army Headquarters. After March 1916 various British divisional headquarters were located here including that of the 47th Division. **Pioneer James Greenwood**, attached to the Special Brigade, Royal Engineers (RE), recalled the nature of their billets here in July 1916: 'The barns and outbuildings swarmed with rats. In our billet, in a barn, our beds were wooden frames with wire netting stretched across. We raised them on bricks so that rats running about during the night would run under the bed. Those that had no such beds had rats running across their beds quite frequently.'

When the Canadians took over the northern sector the chateau became the headquarters of the 4th Canadian Division under the command of **Major General David Watson**. Known by the Canadians as 'Canada Camp', the area in and around the chateau had clearly improved and was a teeming hive of activity during the build-up to the attack on Vimy Ridge. Also in residence here would have been

The entrance gates to the Château de la Haie.

Lieutenant Colonel Edmund Ironside who was serving on the 4th Canadian Division staff as the principal staff officer (GSO1). Ironside would rise to become Chief of the Imperial General Staff in 1940. In March 1917 **Sergeant Leonard Gould**, serving with 102/Battalion CEF, described his stay at the chateau:

> This was our first experience of the newly-constructed camps in the grounds of the Château de la Haie. The latter was a fine stone building standing in beautiful park grounds which had been taken over by the Allies for military purposes. For very many months it was used for Brigade Headquarters by the Divisions operating in the Vimy sector, and in the surrounding grounds there sprang up four camps, known as St Lawrence, Niagara, Canada, and Vancouver. A good bath-house was constructed at the bottom of the slope leading down from the château, and later in the year a fine theatre was built. During the summer the camps around the château were pleasant enough, but in the early days of their being, when the weather was inclement and the accommodation limited, they suffered badly from the mud, which was always well over the boot-tops and frequently engulfed a man to the knees.

You will see a CWGC signpost for Villers Station Cemetery ½km further along the road. An unmetalled track along the disused line of the railway leads past the former station building to the cemetery but pause just before the former railway station.

An information board on the right recalls the former 54km long Tortillard Line – a slow train on a winding route – which opened in 1890 and once linked Lens to Frévent, ferrying miners to the coalfields and transporting produce and coal between rural communities. The line was crucial during the First World War in providing the transport of supplies and the evacuation of casualties. It was also used during the Second World War, even by the Resistance and Miss Gervois, the daughter of the station master, received the Medal of the Resistance for her part in the struggle against the occupying Germans. On one occasion a black marketeer transported a bed loaded with supplies along the line here under the very noses of the Germans! The line finally closed in May 1948.

Continue along the track.

Villers Station Cemetery

This is a large cemetery and within sight of the gates of the Château de la Haie. Originally begun by the French, it was used by Commonwealth divisions and field ambulances from July 1916 until September 1918 and is particularly associated with the Canadian divisions whose graves – dating from April 1917 and the Battle of Vimy Ridge – are in Plots V–X. Enlarged after the Armistice when isolated graves were moved here, the majority of the French graves were removed to the national cemetery at Notre-Dame de Lorette in 1923 but the thirty-two German graves that are marked by one headstone remained. Today there are 1,208 Commonwealth burials in addition to the thirty-two Germans.

A number of casualties incurred during the large-scale Canadian raid of 1 March 1917 are buried here. From the four battalions that took part 687 men were killed, wounded or missing. Sixty-five of the recovered casualties from the raid can be located in Plots, V, VI, VII and VIII, Rows D and E, two of the most notable being 56-year-old **Lieutenant Colonel Arnold Kemball** (VI.E.1), commanding 54/Battalion, and 48-year-old **Lieutenant Colonel Samuel Beckett** (VII.D.1), commanding 75/Battalion. Two majors – **Major Frederick**

Villers Station Cemetery.

Travers Lucas (VI.E.2) of 54/Battalion and **Major James Langstaff** (VII.D.2) of 75/Battalion – were killed in the raid, as was another, 33-year-old **Major Russell Johnston** (V.F.3), who was one of two officers of 72/Battalion killed. Before you leave visit the single headstone situated behind the Cross of Sacrifice which marks the grave of New Zealand-born **Air Mechanic Norman Brain** who was serving with 11 Squadron, RFC. He died of wounds on 22 October 1916, and had most probably been brought in from the squadron airfield at le Hameau to one of the field ambulance units. Le Hameau airfield later became well known as the base from which **Billy Bishop** claimed his forty-seven victories.

A calvary that had stood at the entrance to the village of Carency – *le Christ de Carency* – was badly damaged in 1914, bullet-holed and with both arms being blown off. It was transported here when the Germans were driven from the village and erected in front of a hut next to what was then the French military cemetery. In November 1948, when the Tortillard Line finally closed, *le Christ de Carency* was moved to Notre-Dame de Lorette, where it was erected first in an outdoor niche on the southern wall of the chapel on 11 November that year and then later moved inside where it can be seen today.

Retrace your route back to the main road and as you reach it look straight ahead, across the road, to see the line of the disused railway continuing its course through the wooded Vallée Miclette towards Carency, which we explore in **Route 3**.

Turn right onto the D65 and drive through Villers-au-Bois, where the Divisional Headquarters of the 3rd Canadian Division was situated, until you reach a T-junction. Turn left onto the D58, signposted Carency. Continue on the D58 and after negotiating the right-hand bend in the road the white lantern tower of the French cemetery of Notre-Dame de Lorette comes into view on the high ground to your left. You will soon enter Carency.

Carency

The village was taken by the Germans in October 1914 and they quickly set about establishing it as a strategic strongpoint straddling the D58 Carency–Souchez road to resist any French advance towards Lens. Situated along the slopes of the narrow Carency Valley, in 1914 the village comprised five groups of houses, one in the centre of the village – which included the church – and the other four facing roughly north, south, east and west. The Germans transformed the village into a fortress defended by four lines of trenches. Each street was fortified and connected by subterranean passages, enabling the garrison of four battalions to man the defences quickly. As early as December 1914 the French attempted to take Carency and two attacks on 18 and 27 December brought them to the northern and western outskirts of the village. The subsequent period of mine and counter-mining warfare gradually destroyed the German line and made the western approaches to the village all but impassable. The attack of 9 May 1915, led by **Général Émile Fayolle** and the 70th Division, XXXIII Corps, was directed against the southern and eastern aspects of the village. Finally, after bitter close-quarter fighting, the French finally captured Hill 124 to the northeast whilst to the northwest the deep fortified quarry, which was north of the road to **Moulin Topart**, was also taken. By 12 May the remaining Germans had been surrounded and were compelled to surrender. Not a single building in Carency escaped destruction and all that remained was the 1749 church bell which had been hidden away before the fighting began. It would not ring again until 1928, following the reconstruction of the village, which was completed in 1931.

Drive through Carency, passing the French war memorial on the left to take the next turning on the left, signposted Ablain-St-Nazaire. This is the Rue de Moulin which takes you across the bridge over the tiny *le Carency* river before it climbs gently through a right-hand bend to reach Ablain-St-Nazaire. As you enter the village the lantern tower of Notre-Dame de Lorette is almost directly ahead of you on the high ground. Continue downhill to the T-junction where a right turn onto the D57 will take you for approximately 1.4km to a junction where the ruins of Ablain-St-Nazaire church can be seen on the left. Turn left – signposted Anneau de la Mémoire Lorette and Notre-Dame de Lorette – and park with the church on your left.

Ablain-St-Nazaire and the church

After the fall of Carency the village of Ablain-St-Nazaire was totally destroyed during the battle that ended on 29 May 1915, when the last group of fortified houses was taken in the north of the village on the slopes of Notre-Dame de Lorette. The sixteenth-century church – built by local aristocrat Charles de Bourbon-Carency as a mark of gratitude to St Nazarius for the cure of his daughter's mental illness – was declared an A-Grade historic building in 1908, and it is the ruins of that church which you can see today. The church was designed by architect **Jacques le Caron**, who also conceived the original *Hôtel*

The ruins of the church at Ablain-St-Nazaire stand as a permanent memorial to those who died.

de Ville and *Beffroi* in the Place des Héros in Arras. In 1914, after the Germans had occupied the village, the French artillery destroyed the building to prevent the 34m-high tower being used as an observation post. After the war the Historic Monuments Commission decided against rebuilding the church, preferring to allow the ruins to stand permanently as a memorial to those who had died, making way for a new church to be built on Rue Marcel Landcino, opposite the *Mairie*. As you walk round the shattered walls of the church, bear in mind that it was only the remains of the church tower that you can see today that stood defiantly above the shattered remnants of the village in 1918. On a hot day in late July 1916, the 1908 Olympic rowing gold medallist, composer and pianist **Lieutenant Commander Frederick Kelly DSC**, commanding B Company of the Hood Battalion of the RND, recalled 'rather an interesting ride across the Lorette ridge' on his way to lunch at Hood Battalion headquarters amongst the ruins of Ablain-St-Nazaire. 'Their billets there are under observation from the enemy trenches and in consequence of the men having orders not to show themselves in the street, the village looked very deserted. It was of course in a state of ruin.'

Ablain-St-Nazaire: looking down Rue du Flot with the Lantern Tower of Notre-Dame de Lorette on the skyline.

Return to your vehicle and continue uphill for 130m where a left turn along the steep Rue de la Blanche Voie will take you to Notre-Dame de Lorette. Bear right at the top of the road and, keeping the cemetery on your left, park by the southern entrance to the cemetery.

Notre-Dame de Lorette

Ablain-St-Nazaire is dominated to the north by the crest of the long Notre-Dame de Lorette spur which extends from **Bouvigny Wood** in the west to the north of **Souchez** in the east. In 1914, at the top of the spur, close to the modern day Ring of Remembrance, was the chapel of Notre-Dame de Lorette, the venue for a popular religious pilgrimage. Whilst the northern slopes of the spur are relatively gentle, those on the southern side are steep. Seen from Ablain-St-Nazaire, five steep, stubby fingered spurs separated by steep ravines run down from the Notre-Dame plateau into the valley below – christened the Côtes de Melon by the French infantry – and each had to be taken in turn. Led by **Général Maistre's XXI Corps**, which gained a foothold on the most westerly of the ridges, the Éperon de

Mathis, was captured after heavy fighting in December 1914 and January 1915. The second ridge – le Grand Éperon – was taken on 15 March 1915 by the 158th Regiment of Infantry after capturing three trench lines and beating back strong counter-attacks. The third – l'Éperon des Arabes – was taken in April in preparation for the larger May offensive. The approach road you have just travelled along takes its name from the fourth spur – Éperon de la Blanche Voie – and gives the visitor at least a fleeting impression of the sheer enormity of the task faced by the French infantry when ordered to attack the heights of this series of spurs.

On 9 May during the Second Battle of Artois, three infantry regiments fought through five lines of trenches to close the last 1,000m to the small chapel that gave the plateau its name. By the time the fighting ended on 13 May, the ground was littered with dead and dying soldiers, and the small chapel was completely destroyed. Four months later on 25 September 1915, during the Third Battle of Artois, Maistre's XXI Corps pushed down into the outskirts of Souchez and **Général Marie Fayolle's XXXIII Corps** took the fortified **Château de Carleul** and Souchez Communal Cemetery. The French Official History concludes the account of the battle thus: 'The Germans were beaten and the chapel, in ruins, was left behind. Beyond was an inextricable, chaotic tangle of underground passages and shelters, mine craters and shell holes, encumbered with dead, arms and equipment and stores.' The plateau remained much the same until work started in 1920 to create a permanent monument to the dead. In 1916 **Lieutenant Guy Chapman**, serving with 13/Royal Fusiliers at Coupigny, was greeted by a tragic stillness and a picture that remained etched upon his mind:

A grisly graveyard of fallen trenches and mangled bones, nameless, unrecorded … As I stood beside a crumbling ditch, filled with helmets, long rifles, and these somehow less than human bones, a heavy piece of earth, grass grown, fell, loosened by the rain, from the top. In the cavity lay something that had once been blue, faded to fleece colour, stained with earth.

The first stones of the Lantern Tower and Chapel were laid on 19 June 1921, with the major structural work continuing until the end of the 1930s. During the work, a temporary chapel made from sheet metal was constructed nearby for the annual pilgrimages which had resumed in 1919. A registry office was also set up in order to provide information to the families who came here to mourn the dead.

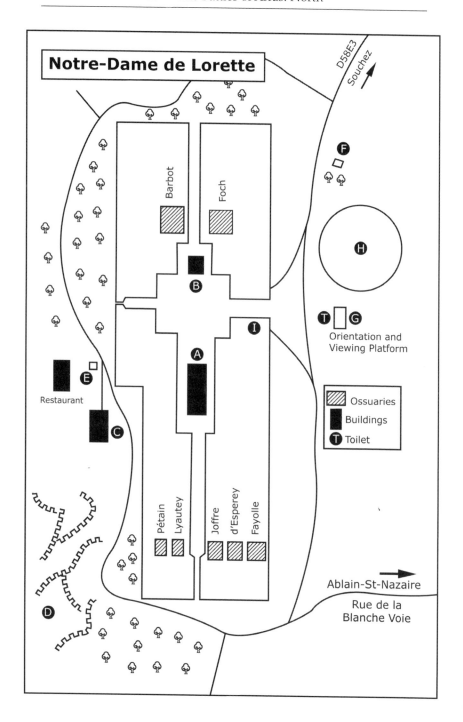

Notre-Dame de Lorette

D58E3
Souchez

F

Barbot

Foch

H

B

T G

Orientation and
Viewing Platform

I

A

E

Restaurant

C

	Ossuaries
	Buildings
T	Toilet

Pétain Lyautey

Joffre d'Esperey Fayolle

D

Ablain-St-Nazaire

Rue de la
Blanche Voie

Once you have arrived at the top, the high ground of Vimy Ridge is only about 5km away to the southeast, revealing much of the battlefield across the Souchez Valley and highlighting the strategic importance of this ground. We suggest you refer to the cemetery plan to navigate yourself around the site and decide for yourself exactly what you wish to see.

There are public toilets ❶ situated below the orientation and viewing platform ❻ opposite the main entrance to the cemetery as well as in the restaurant.

The Original Chapel of Notre-Dame de Lorette

Built on the plateau overlooking Ablain-St-Nazaire in 1727 and financed by **Florent Guilbert**, a painter from the village who was miraculously cured after a pilgrimage to the Italian hill town of Lorreto, the chapel quickly developed into a centre of pilgrimage. Destroyed in 1794 and rebuilt in 1815, it was enlarged between 1870 and 1880. During the construction work for the Ring of Remembrance, the building's foundations were uncovered, confirming the location of Guilbert's original chapel, which is also marked by a small plaque on the ground just inside the main entrance.

The Cemetery

This is the largest of the French National Cemeteries, covering an area of 13 hectares. At first sight the sheer size of the cemetery can overwhelm the visitor if they wander into the sea of white crosses which appears almost endless. Today, 40,057 soldiers from four conflicts have their final resting place here, although the 19,998 casualties from the First World War vastly outnumber those from other conflicts. The visitor will notice the seven ossuaries – to either end of the cemetery – which contain the remains of French soldiers brought in from the Artois battlefields, including single burials, burials in civilian cemeteries and small military burial sites within a radius of some 45km of Ablain-St-Nazaire. The ossuaries are all named after French military commanders, and an eighth ossuary can be found at the base of the Lantern Tower. Each of the identified casualties is marked by a white concrete cross and casualties that were killed on a particular battlefield are, as far as possible, buried together in the same section. Muslim and Jewish casualties are buried separately, in the western end of the cemetery, each of the Muslim graves being positioned to face east. Initially, the crosses marking each grave were constructed from wood but these were gradually replaced by more durable concrete in the early 1930s. The grave of **Général Ernest Barbot**, commanding the

The Modern Chapel of Notre-Dame de Lorette and the Lantern Tower.

French 77th Division, ❶ is on the left as you enter the cemetery (grave 19293). It was originally marked with a cross made out of shell casings. Stolen in 1952, it was replaced with the same simple cross that marks the final resting place of so many of Barbot's comrades in arms. At the far end of the same row are the graves of a father and son: Hungarian-born **Lajos de Sars**, killed in September 1915, and **Edmond de Sars**, killed at Valenciennes in May 1940.

Ernest Barbot is buried amongst the men of the 77th Division.

The Modern Chapel of Notre-Dame de Lorette Ⓐ
The modern chapel was designed by **Louis-Marie Cordonnier** and is sited about 100m from the location of the original chapel destroyed during the war. The building was blessed in the presence of Maréchal Pétain on 26 May 1927 and consecrated on 5 September 1937. The building has retained the term 'chapel'

even though it is quite a grand structure in the Romano-Byzantine style and is often referred to as the Basilica. The structure is made of a cement frame with a stone facing, much of it sourced from the rubble of Béthune and the dismantled walls of Lille. Inside, the walls are covered with hundreds of memorial plaques dedicated to units and individuals and the eagle-eyed amongst you will spot the plaque, to the right of the entrance, dedicated to Luxembourg-born **François Faber**, who won the Tour de France in 1909 and was killed near Berthonval on 9 May 1915, serving with the French Foreign Legion. During the 1909 race he won five consecutive stages which remains a record to this day. There is also a memorial to **Louise de Bettignies** who became a British and French spy working under the names 'Alice Dubois' and 'Pauline'. In October 1915 she was arrested in Tournai and sentenced to death, a verdict that was eventually commuted to a prison term. After being transferred to Sieburg she died of pneumonia in September 1918. Within the glass case you can see the original wooden cross placed on her grave in Cologne Cemetery. She was posthumously awarded the Croix de la Guerre, Légion d'Honneur, the British Military Medal and the Order of the British Empire.

The stained glass windows were created by Charles Loris from designs by Hénri Pinta and depict the coats of arms of Arras, Boulogne-sur-Mer and St Omer together with several historical French personages and scenes from the First World War. The six windows donated by the British Empire in thanks for the land given by France for British cemeteries were created by Henry Payne at the instigation of British Prime Minister, **Stanley Baldwin**, and were unveiled in August 1929. The first chaplain of the Chapel of Notre-Dame de Lorette was **Léon Briche** (1884–1936) and his grave can be found amongst the trees near the eastern edge of the site.

The Lantern Tower ❸

Designed by Louis-Marie Cordonnier, the tower is 52m high and stands opposite the entrance to the chapel. At the time of writing it was not possible to climb to the viewing platform which was closed to the public for reasons of security. After dark the beacon from the Lantern Tower revolves five times each minute, its ray of light seen at a distance of some 70km. At the base of the tower there is an ossuary and a chapel of rest, where, amongst a number of other coffins, there are three which contain the remains of unknown soldiers from the Second World War, the North African War and the Indo-China Wars. In April 1955 a container containing soil and ashes from the

Second World War concentration camps was lodged here. Finally, it is worth visiting the small museum, which you will find up a set of steps, which contains personal items and describes the history of the construction. The **Eternal Flame** sits between the Chapel and the Lantern Tower.

The Musée Vivant, 1914–18 **C**

You will find the museum on the northern edge of the site, close to the **Estaminet de Lorette**, which gives the visitor the opportunity for a well-deserved rest and refreshments. Be advised that the toilets are for customers only. The museum, which is open every day from 9.00am to 8.00pm, February to December, contains displays of French and German equipment and five full-sized scenes of life in the trenches. Entrance to the museum at the time of writing was €5. For a further €1 (buy a disc from the museum to access the gate) the visitor can inspect several examples of large artillery pieces, including a rusted German 245mm trench mortar, a French 155mm Schneider artillery piece and a German 77mm gun. Further on, shell craters identify no-man's-land with reconstructed French trenches to the west and German trenches to the east. **D** Both trench lines exhibit numerous firing positions and wire obstacles and are on the

A French 75mm field gun is amongst the Musée Vivrant's outdoor display.

actual ground where the fighting for the final section of the crest took place. Near the museum is the memorial to 24-year-old **Sous Lieutenant Hénri Merlin** who was killed on 3 March 1915 whilst serving with 10th Chasseurs á Pied. ❺ Refusing to surrender, he killed himself rather than be taken prisoner.

The International Memorial 'Ring of Remembrance' ❻
The latest addition to the Notre-Dame de Lorette site is situated by the main entrance to the cemetery and close to the orientation platform where access is gained via a short tunnel. Designed by architect **Phillipe Prost**, the giant elliptical memorial was inaugurated on 11 November 2014 by the then President of the French Republic, François Hollande. The outside of the 328m ring,

The memorial to Sous Lieutenant Hénri Merlin.

which appears to hover over the plateau here, is formed by a dark, lightweight concrete wall, whilst the inside is adorned with 500 plates of bronzed and burnished stainless steel on which are engraved the names of the 579,606 casualties of all nationalities – male and female – who fell on the Western Front during the First World War. Part of the structure uses a cantilever overhang to symbolize the fragility of peace. The names of the dead have been inscribed in alphabetical order, Philippe Prost's intention being to 'give shape to brotherhood' and to 'unite yesterday's enemies'. He chose the ring as 'a figure to bring together the names of the soldiers, thinking of the circle formed by people holding hands. The ring is synonymous with unity and eternity: unity, because the names form a sort of human chain, and eternity because the letters are joined without an end, in alphabetical order without any distinction of nationality, rank or religion.' Amongst the myriad names engraved on the memorial you will find **François Faber**, winner of the 1909 Tour de France; **Walter Tull**, one of the British Army's first black officers; **Simon Fraser**, the inspiration for the Australian Cobber Memorial at Fromelles; **John Kipling**, son of the poet and writer Rudyard Kipling; **Joseph Standing Buffalo**, grandson of the Indian Chief Sitting Bull; **Hans Dülfer**, the German alpinist credited with more than forty first ascents; and **Paul Mauk**,

The Ring of Remembrance.

the youngest enlisted German soldier, who was 14 years old when he was killed in June 1915. To check whether a name is engraved inside the ring, a smart-phone application in English is available to download: *Anneau de la Memoire Notre-Dame de Lorette*. The memorial is open every day from 9.00am until 4.00pm in the winter months and 5.30pm in summer.

Association of Notre-Dame de Lorette Monument
The Association was founded in 1920 with the principal aims of keeping alive the memory of the dead of all wars and the upkeep of the cemetery. There are over 3,000 members who include founder members and associated members who assist with access and information for visitors. The Guarde d'Honneur de Lorette are volunteers who retain the memory of those who died for France and are representatives of the families of the dead who are known to be buried in the cemetery. Each day of the year between Palm Sunday and 11 November, the Honour Guards stand guard at the chapel and on each Sunday at 11.45am the Eternal Flame is rekindled by the leader of the guards on duty that day.

The Statue of Général Paul Maistre (1858–1922)

This statue, which was unveiled in May 1927, stands on the spot where it is thought he had his command post in May 1915. Born in 1858, he was 57 years old when the French 21st Division finally took the plateau of Notre-Dame de Lorette. Despite his subsequent promotion and command of the French Sixth Army, he will always be associated with the battles to regain control of the Notre-Dame de Lorette plateau. From his statue the views over the Souchez Valley open up, and apart from excellent views of the two *crassiers* on the Loos battlefield, Vimy Ridge and the Canadian Memorial can be made out in the distance.

Général Paul Maistre, who commanded XXI Corps de Armée.

Leave the site and drive downhill. At the T-junction you will see the **Musée Lens 1914–18** directly ahead of you. The museum is open from Tuesday to Sunday from 10.00am to 7.00pm. Guided tours are organized by the Lens-Liévin Tourist and Heritage Office.

At the junction turn right – signposted Arras Centre Ville – and continue through Souchez on the D937 for approximately 1km. Turn right just before the *Mairie* onto the D57, signposted Ablain-St-Nazaire.

In 1916 this road junction formed part of the track known as **Duck Walk** and was frequently used by **Frederick Kelly** when the Hood Battalion of the RND was occupying the trenches at Souchez. On 31 July 1916 he wrote: 'I spent the remaining time till morning stand-to-arms in going round my line and in reconnoitring Duck Walk back to battalion headquarters across the open – about 400 yards long – and going out with a patrol of two men who have to patrol from the right of my line to a bombing station down by the Souchez river.'

Drive for approximately 500m along the D57 to find a large white building on the right, which was the former station restaurant. On the left is a long driveway marked by two bollards with a minor road and car parking to its right. The private driveway will take you to

The former railway line from which the French attacked the Château de Carleul defences.

the rebuilt **Château de Carleul**, which was taken by the French on 25 September 1915. The attack was begun from the embankment of the former Lens–Frévent railway line, which ran west of the chateau, and is now the minor road where you are parked. This road quickly becomes an unmetalled track and, unfortunately, the chateau and grounds are screened from view by a line of trees, but it was from this very line that the French attack on the heavily fortified chateau took place. The French Official history describes the advance made by Général Fayolle's 70th Division:

> At the appointed time the Chasseurs dashed across the railway which separated them from the Park of Carleul. By means of folding footbridges, they crossed the moats of the château and entered the park. The Germans gave way under the violence of the shock, and a mad pursuit began over the muddy ground, across the swamps, mine craters, labyrinths of trenches and fallen trees.

If you walk down the minor road for a short distance – note the old station building – you should be able to look across to the right for views of the two churches in Ablain-St-Nazaire.

Retrace your route and return towards Souchez to the junction with the D937. Be mindful that the ancient town which had flourished prior to 1914 was completely destroyed along with its two railway stations, thirteenth-century stone cross and fifteenth-century church. The plinth of the stone cross is one of the few pre-war relics still visible in the village and stands today on the corner of Rue Pasteur and Rue Currie across the road and to the left opposite the junction. Turn right to continue through Souchez, which finally fell to the French on 26 September 1915.

After 600m the road begins to rise and you will see a triangular glass sculpture on the right and, almost immediately afterwards, the statue of Général Ernest Barbot set back from the road. There is parking behind the memorial.

The Ernest Barbot Memorial
Designed by Jules Déchin, work began in 1935 and the memorial was inaugurated in May 1937. The statue is dedicated to Barbot and his men of the 77th Division who fell in Artois between October 1914 and February 1916. Barbot stands as if leading his men into battle with his left hand between the buttons of his greatcoat – note the

The Barbot Memorial.

numerals 159 denoting his original regiment on his collar; his right hand appears to be pointing towards his soldiers, who can be seen climbing out of their trenches behind him. On either side of the monument are two plaques, one commemorating **Général Louis Plessier**, who preceded Barbot as commander of the 77th Division and died of wounds after the Battle of Mulhouse in 1914. Contrary to popular opinion, Barbot was not the first French general to be killed in action, but was the first to receive mortal wounds from which he subsequently died. The second plaque commemorates the short-lived command of **Général Jean Paul Stirn**, who, as Barbot's successor, was killed two days later.

Général **Ernest Barbot**
Born in 1855, Barbot graduated from St Cyr in 1877; fifteen years later he was commanding the 159th Regiment of Alpine Infantry in Briançon and by 1914 he was in command of the 77th Division, known amongst his men as the 'Division Barbot' and was transferred to the Artois front. In May 1915, the French launched their campaign against Notre-Dame de Lorette and Vimy. Barbot's men took Hill 119, which later became known by the Canadians as 'The Pimple', Givenchy-en-Gohelle and the outskirts of Souchez. Sadly, the speed of the advance proved to be their undoing and they were forced back as far as the site of a small estaminet called **Cabaret Rouge**, near the location of the present-day CWGC cemetery. Establishing his headquarters in a trench, Barbot was hit by shrapnel whilst running across open ground. He died later whilst in the dressing station at Villers-Châtel. The 77th went on to take Souchez in September but Vimy Ridge and the Douai Plain remained in the hands of the Germans.

The North African Memorial
The memorial was erected to commemorate the 700 officers and men who were killed in North Africa between 1952 and 1964. Inaugurated in September 2002, the central pathway is aligned through the Barbot Memorial towards Notre-Dame de Lorette, where the Unknown Soldier from the North African War lies in the lantern tower. The twelve trees that surround the memorial garden represent the twelve years of the conflict.

Leave the memorial and continue uphill to find the CWGC sign for Cabaret Rouge Cemetery. The road curves to the right and the German line of 1915 hugged the curve to the left of the road. Drive slowly as about 100m further up the road on the left is a small plaque at ground level erected by the Association le Souvenir Français in 2002. This purports to mark the location of the original Cabaret Rouge estaminet, although the exact site was about 100m further up the road on the left, almost on the bend; not a good spot to position a memorial!

The red-brick Cabaret Rouge café gave its name to this sector of the front line and a nearby communication trench. It was destroyed by shellfire in March 1915 but its cellar had been turned into a strongpoint by the Germans. It was a bitterly contested position and remained in German hands after the offensive of May–June 1915 until Souchez was finally cleared in the autumn. The French soldier and author Hénri Barbusse noted in October 1915 that there was 'nothing left' of Cabaret Rouge, 'the rubble heaped there is red like the brick which made the home, when it was a home'. In his novel *Le Feu* (1916) he called on his grisly memories of a German corpse with a head like a cat in the 'flat field tiled with broken bricks' around Cabaret Rouge: 'And what is that?' … not a milestone. It is a head, a black head, tanned and waxed. The mouth is crooked, and we see the moustache that bristles on either side: a large scorched cat's head. The body – a German – is underneath, buried upright.' Another tableau formed 'a gloomy scene … a skull, all white, and two meters from the skull, a pair of boots, and, between the two, a heap of frayed leather and rags cemented by brown mud.

Continue to the cemetery ahead.

Cabaret Rouge British Cemetery
This is a very large CWGC cemetery that was first used by Commonwealth units in March 1916. Given the size of the plot, it is easy to become overwhelmed by the sheer number of headstones confronting you on arrival. Whatever the reason for your visit, this is a cemetery that draws you back time and again to wander amongst the now tranquil rows of those who made the ultimate sacrifice. One of the first things you may notice is the plaque erected in the entrance shelter to the former Canadian Army officer **Frank Higginson**, who designed the cemetery whilst working as an architect for the IWGC in the 1920s and later acted as Secretary to the Commission.

Cabaret Rouge British Cemetery.

The cemetery was used mostly by the 47th (London) Division and the Canadian Corps until August 1917 and by other units until September 1918. It was greatly enlarged after the war when as many as 7,000 graves were concentrated here from over 100 other cemeteries. For much of the twentieth century, Cabaret Rouge served as one of a small number of 'open cemeteries' in which the remains of servicemen newly discovered in the region were buried. Today the cemetery contains over 7,650 burials of the First World War, over half of which remain unidentified.

Readers of our guidebook *The Battles of French Flanders* will recognize the name of 25-year-old **Second Lieutenant Henry Noel Atkinson** (XIII.E.12), whose memorial can be found in Violaines Communal Cemetery, near La Bassée. Atkinson's body was discovered in 1923 and buried in the cemetery here, leaving the memorial at Violaines where it can still be seen today. Serving with 1/Cheshires, he was involved in the fighting at Audregnies and during the subsequent Retreat from Mons in 1914. Another officer, whose death we describe in *The Battles of French Flanders*, is **Lieutenant Colonel Victor Rickard** (XXVII.A.14). Rickard was commanding 2/Munster Fusiliers during the Battle of Aubers Ridge and was killed southeast of the Rue du Bois on 9 May 1915 when he was hit by a bullet in the spinal column. **Lieutenant Charles van Neck** (XVI.B.17), aged 21, was serving with 1/Northumberland Fusiliers when he was killed on 20 October 1914 by a sniper on the II Corps front line near La Bassée. Charles van Neck was a cousin of Second Lieutenant John Le Steere, who was killed at Zillebeke serving with 2/Grenadier Guards on 17 November 1914. The unfortunate Van Neck family was soon to hear of the death in action of their eldest son, 27-year-old **Lieutenant Phillip van Neck**, who was killed serving with 1/Grenadier Guards at Gheluvelt, near Ypres on 26 October 1914. We refer to Phillip's grave at Zantvoorde British Cemetery and John Le Steere's non-standard headstone at Zillebeke in our guidebook *Ypres – Nieuwpoort to Ploegsteert*.

The cemetery contains numerous graves of British, Irish, Australian, New Zealand, Indian and South African soldiers and is also the final resting place of over seventy officers of the RFC and Royal Air Force (RAF). Two of these men are 25-year-old **Second Lieutenant Morden Mowat** (XVI.D.4) and **Second Lieutenant Clarence Rogers** (XVI.D.6) who were both shot down by the German air ace **Max Immelmann**. Mowat was flying a Bristol Scout from 11 Squadron on 16 May 1916 when he was shot down. Sadly, he died of wounds behind the German lines. Rogers was flying a FE2b from 25 Squadron and was shot down on 18 June 1916. Rogers' observer, Sergeant Taylor, was wounded but survived to be taken prisoner. It was during this same engagement, involving several British and German machines, that Immelmann was killed. His brother Franz and German Sixth Army experts concluded that he had died as a consequence of shooting the propeller from his Fokker EIII Eindecker following the failure of his aircraft's machine-gun interrupter gear. Anonymous 'eyewitnesses' quoted in the press claimed, however, that Immelmann's machine broke up, whilst another – *Offizierstellvertreter* Hugo Gropp, of the 2nd *Kompanie*, RIR 76 – talks of a mid-air explosion.

Also buried here are two poets who were cut down before their work could achieve its full potential: 22-year-old **Second Lieutenant Robert Beckh** (Marquillies Communal Cemetery, German Ext Memorial 24) is buried to the left of the entrance. He was killed serving with 12/East Yorkshires on 15 August 1916. His best known work is contained in the posthumous volume *Swallows in Storm and Sunlight*. The second is 35-year-old **Captain Charles John Beech Masefield** (VI.H.23), who was killed on 2 July 1917 and was a cousin of John Masefield, who later became Poet Laureate. A solicitor by profession, Charles' verse has been very much overshadowed by his cousin's literary achievements, although he did write a novel in 1908 and a volume of poems in 1911 entitled *The Seasons' Difference and Other Poems*. His final poetic work was published posthumously in 1919. Killed near Lens, his body was brought into the cemetery after the Armistice.

Cabaret Rouge has a particularly close connection with the Canadian Infantry, and the visitor will find thirty identified casualties killed on 9 April 1917 during the Battle of Vimy Ridge. Two of these men were brothers serving with the Royal Canadian Regiment, killed together on the same day. **Private Wilfred Chenier** (XII.E.15) and **Private Olivier Chenier** (XII.E.16) now lie together in death. Many visitors will know that it was from this cemetery that the remains of the **Canadian Unknown Soldier** (VIII.E.7) were removed on 16 May 2000 and flown to Canada to be reinterred in a coffin of Silver Maple wood in a tomb in front of the National War Memorial in Ottowa nine days later. The soldier was killed on 9 April 1917 whilst serving with 87/Battalion and a special headstone in the cemetery commemorates the event.

After leaving the cemetery turn right and continue for 1.6km until you reach the Czech Memorial (*Cimetière Militaire Tchécoslovaque*) on the right and the Polish Memorial (*Memorial des Polonaise*) on the left. There is parking by the entrance.

Captain Charles Masefield.

The headstone marking the former grave of the unknown Canadian soldier.

The Czech Memorial and Cemetery

From the steps of the cemetery it is possible to see Notre-Dame de Lorette and across to Vimy Ridge, where the top of the two pylons of the Canadian War Memorial can be seen on Hill 145. Many Czechs – ethnic minority exiles from the Austro-Hungarian Empire living in France – volunteered to join the 2nd Marching Regiment of the French Foreign Legion in August 1914. The regiment formed part of the Moroccan Division fighting

The Czech Memorial.

in the May 1915 Artois offensive, when they captured this area sustaining heavy casualties. The memorial was erected in 1925 and is linked specifically to the action of 9 May 1915 when the Czechs attacked the German strongpoint at **Thélus Mill** and gained the summit of **Vimy Ridge**, during which 70 men were killed and around 150 wounded. After the war the Association of the Czechoslovakian Volunteers of France was created and the memorial was unveiled in May 1925. It was not until 1958, however, that the Association of the Czechoslovakian Volunteers was able to create the cemetery that you see now; 206 graves (70 from the First World War and 136 from the Second World War) from 73 cemeteries were successively brought here and reinterred. The official opening of the cemetery took place in May 1963 and the last burials were transferred in 1970. In the centre of the cemetery stands a **Bohemian Cross**, a reminder of the death of John of Luxembourg, King of Bohemia, who died fighting alongside the King of France during the Battle of Crecy in 1346. A commemorative ceremony is held here each year at the beginning of May.

The Polish Memorial
Across the road is the Polish Memorial. Take great care when crossing the carriageway as it can be very busy with fast-moving traffic. Poland had existed as a kingdom before its partition at the end of the eighteenth century and this memorial commemorates the Polish volunteers who, like the Czechs, had enlisted in the 2nd Marching Regiment of the Foreign Legion and who also fell on 9 May 1915 during the attack on **Vimy Ridge**. At the beginning of the war about 2,000 Poles fought under the French flag as many had settled in Artois and worked in the mines around Douai. The monument was designed by **Maxime Real del Sarte** and inaugurated in May 1933 in the presence of the Polish Ambassador to France. Seven years later the Germans destroyed the monument and it was rebuilt after the Second World War only to suffer damage again during a storm in 1967. The monument you see today was rebuilt with money raised by subscriptions from the Polish community.

Continue for another 1.2km until you reach a crossroads with the D49. On the right is a museum, whilst on the left is the La Targette Memorial or, as it is more commonly known, the Torch of Peace. We suggest you turn left at the crossroads where there is parking on the left-hand side of the road.

The Polish Memorial.

The Torch of Peace Memorial and the Cité des Mutilés
The monument was constructed in 1930 and inaugurated on 20 October 1932. The sculpture depicts the hand of a soldier – grasping a flaming torch raised above the 'fields of sacrifice' – thrusting out of the ruins of Neuville-St-Vaast, symbolizing rebirth after the destruction wrought by war. On either side are two private memorials which have been brought in from fields to the north of the village. On the left a sculptured stone cross commemorates the death of **Lieutenant Hénri Millevoye** who was killed serving with 24th Regiment of Infantry on 25 September 1915, whilst on the right a second cross commemorates the death of Toulon born **Sous Lieutenant Charles Nouette-d'Andrezel** of the 36th Regiment of Infantry on the same date.

Running east from the crossroads is Rue du 11 Novembre, where for many years a memorial concrete archway spanned the road marking the entrance to the **Cité des Mutilés**. Created by **Ernest Petit** (1889–1964), a Notary Public and philanthropist who also initiated the reconstruction of Neuville-St-Vaast, a plaque dedicated

The Torch of Peace.

The cross commemorating the death of Lieutenant Hénri Millevoye.

to his memory can be found in front of the Torch of Peace Memorial, which he also raised. It was Petit who created the commune's postwar *blason* – coat of arms – in 1921, incorporating the *Croix de Guerre* and the inscription '9 mai 1915' – the date of the start of Neuville's liberation but also its complete destruction – and '*Resurgam*' ('I shall rise again') – beneath a Phoenix rising from the ashes. Today the arch has long gone and all that exists of the Cité des Mutilés are the sixteen houses – pavillons – which, as you travel along it, line the left-hand

The plaque dedicated to the memory of Ernest Petit.

The Pavillon Balfourier on Rue du 11 Novembre.

La Croix du Souvenir has been erected by an old communication trench.

side of Rue du 11 Novembre. When the French war cemeteries were constructed, their care was placed in the hands of disabled veterans, a thankless task that saw them living in quite pitiable conditions amongst the ruined towns and villages. Ernest Petit created the Cité des Mutilés to cater for the needs of these men and their families. Each house was built in a different style and allocated to their new owners for a fifth of their market value. As you walk along the street you will see that almost every house was given the name of a military commander with connections to the Neuville sector, whilst the fifty-two mountain ash trees that line the road were planted in honour of the fifty-two men of Neuville-St-Vaast who lost their lives in the war.

On the corner of Rue Jan Tison you will see the house named after **Général Louis d'Armau de Pouydraguin**, who commanded the French 47th Division. He lost two of his sons – Augustin and Jacques – within three days of each other in the Second Battle of Artois in May 1915. They lie together today in the French Military Cemetery at **Maroeuil**: Row 1, Graves 2 and 3.

Continue along the road for another 100m to find a large calvary – La Croix du Souvenir – at the road junction on the right. Erected by an old communication trench, the site has an information panel explaining the origins of the Cité des Mutilés. After you retrace your route to the crossroads reflect on the words of **Pioneer James Greenwood**, who recalled that the La Targette crossroads in March 1917 was a place to be avoided: 'How appropriate a name that was, for the enemy had really plastered it with shellfire. It is a wonder our lorries and their human freight were not blown to smithereens, but fortunately none was hit.'

If you wish you can visit the private museum – owned by the Bardiaux family who also own the museum at Notre-Dame de Lorette – on the opposite corner to the Torch of Peace. It is open every day from 9.00am to 7.00pm. The entrance fee was €4 at the time of writing.

Drive along the D937 for another 400m until you reach the major crossroads with the D55, the CWGC signpost for La Targette British Cemetery is on the right-hand side just before the crossroads. This is the Aux-Rietz crossroads, the site of a tiny hamlet in 1914 but now swallowed up by the southern expansion of La Targette. There are two cemeteries here, the British cemetery and the larger French cemetery, the entrance to which is another 250m further along the road.

La Targette British Cemetery

The cemetery, formerly known as Aux-Rietz Military Cemetery, was begun at the end of April 1917 and used by field ambulances and fighting units until September 1918. Nearly a third of the graves have an artillery connection. After the Armistice sixteen graves were brought into the cemetery from the surrounding battlefields. The cemetery contains 638 First World War burials, 41 of them unidentified. One of the most interesting burials is that of 25-year-old **Lieutenant Colonel Auriol Lowry** (IV.C.1) who was killed on 23 September 1918 whilst in command of 2/West Yorkshires. Captured south of the River Somme during the British withdrawal in March 1918, he escaped from his escort and made his way back to British lines, at one point masquerading as a German soldier and joining an enemy column before slipping away into the darkness. It was a feat that earned him the award of the DSO. In May of that year his battalion was once again embroiled in the fighting on the Aisne where he was wounded. His luck ran out when he was hit by machine-gun fire whilst visiting outposts. Lowry also lost two of his brothers. Patrick, serving as a captain in the same battalion, was killed two days later, William had been killed at Gallipoli in June 1915.

Nearly half the identified casualties here are Canadians and of these there are five graves of men from the Canadian 2nd Division Ammunition Column who were all killed in the same incident on 10 May 1917. The inscription on the headstone marking the grave of **Gunner Percy Allaby** (II.A.15) from Saint John in New Brunswick may have been taken from the last words he ever utttered: 'Do what you can for the rest'. The four other men who were killed with him, very probably as a result of shellfire, are buried nearby.

Next door to the British cemetery is the much larger **French National Cemetery** which opened in 1919 and covers an area of more than 4 hectares. Buried here are the remains of 12,210 officers and men, of whom 11,443 fell in the Battles of Artois. Those that could be identified have individual graves whilst 3,883 unidentified soldiers are buried in 2 mass graves to the rear of the cemetery. A further concentration of graves in 1956 brought in soldiers and members of the Resistance from the Pas de Calais. On the right-hand side there is a large Muslim plot with headstones rather than crosses. In 1935 the French authorities appear to have taken a different course to the British regarding the number of military cemeteries that they were prepared to maintain. Consequently, in the Pas de Calais region, several smaller cemeteries were closed in favour of the five large National Military Cemeteries you can see today.

Leave the cemetery and retrace your steps to the crossroads. Turn right and park your vehicle.

The Aux Reitz Cave
In the period March to April 1917, the 2nd Canadian and 5th Division Artillery had their headquarters in a deep cave system at Aux-Rietz where there was also an ADS. The entrance to the cave is to the right of the car hard standing, directly opposite the restaurant (at the time

of writing this was called Le Relais St Vaast) on the corner of Chemin de Maroeuil and the D937; but the cave has not been open to the public for some time and there is still some concern about the two new houses that have been built over the cave on what was waste ground. That said, there is still a very substantial cave beneath the surface which was originally used for the quarrying of chalk for building stone and during the war it housed hundreds of troops. The regimental historian of the Civil Service Rifles felt that:

> No place on the entire British front could have been more secure from air raids and shellfire than the Aux Rietz Cave. Down wooden steps for over a hundred feet the weary infantryman stumbled, and finally a wonderful underground world presented itself. A large cave capable of holding a thousand men with hundreds of small candles lighting its sombre darkness was the new home to the battalion.

Cornwall-born Harry Trounce was a graduate of the Colorado School of Mines in the United States and a naturalized American citizen. He had joined 175 Tunnelling Company, RE and recalled the cave soon after his arrival on the sector in May 1916:

> We had plenty room for 400 or 500 men, and for a long time it took care of over a thousand ... As it was over 70 feet deep, there was no loss of sleep from enemy shelling ... Stories were current as to a big fight that had occurred down in this cavern in the previous September, and I should judge that there was some truth in the report, on account of the large French cemetery at the crossroads above and the number of bodies we unearthed below in the cavern.

Continue along the D937 for approximately 800m to the entrance to the German cemetery, which you will see on your left. There is ample parking outside the entrance building.

Neuville-St-Vaast German Cemetery (Maison Blanche)
This is the largest of the German First World War cemeteries in France and was created by the French authorities between 1919 and 1923 as they cleared the German dead buried in 110 French communes in the area. The cemetery is situated on ground that was previously known

as the **Labyrinth**, a German defensive position which lay between the villages of Neuville-St-Vaast and Écurie. The name Maison Blanche was adopted from a nearby farm of that name. Beneath the farm is another large cave system – a *souterraine* – which had its origins in providing building stone but was used by Allied troops in both wars. The caves are on private property and access to the public is prohibited. French efforts to take the Labyrinth began on 9 May 1915 and by 16 June, after a protracted offensive, the position was finally overcome. According to a company commander in the 97th Regiment of Infantry, the Labyrinth was:

> An agglomeration of sacks of earth and cement, forming several miles of trenches and boyaux [passageways] which intersected one another in all directions and led to deep underground shelters. Flanked with concrete redoubts and blockhouses, protected by deep entanglements of barbed wire, the place was defended by guns under cupolas, and by machine guns placed at intervals of twenty metres.

The cemetery covers more than 7 hectares and contains the remains of 44,833 German soldiers, of whom 8,040 are buried in a mass grave. Like all German cemeteries the ground is designed to blend into the surroundings and much of the area is planted with trees to evoke the forests of German mythology that watched over the warrior dead. Most of the casualties buried here appear to have fallen during the Battles of Artois early in the war, whilst some fell during the spring of 1917 on Vimy Ridge and others in the autumn of 1918. When the A26 Autoroute was being constructed through the Vimy area more remains of German soldiers were discovered and reinterred here. Two German officers who were killed during a trench raid carried out by 11/Royal Scots, near the present-day Bailleul Road West Cemetery, are buried here. *Leutnant* **Friedrich Haas** rests in Block 17, Grave 563 and *Leutnant* **Alfred Teichmann** is close by in Grave 567. Both men were killed with 6 *Kompanie*, RIR 104, in the savage close-quarter fighting that characterized this trench raid. Visitors will be drawn to the memorial commemorating the men of the Hanoverian Infantry Regiment 164, which was moved here from one of the cleared cemeteries at Boiry-Sainte-Rictrude. Before you leave ponder the impressions of **Private John Boynton Priestley** – later to become famous as J.B. Priestley, the renowned Yorkshire-born author and playwright – when his battalion, 10/Duke of Wellington's, took over the Labyrinth from the French in March 1916:

The German Cemetery at Neuville-St-Vaast.

Into the Labyrinth we went, relieving *poilus* who obviously looked relieved. These were old trenches that had been simply wired off, and when we explored them we found them filled with bloodstained clothing, abandoned equipment, heads, legs and arms. Further on, in a trench still open, several of us, late at night, crawled into the nearest dugout, and soon went to sleep, although the straw in there hardly protected us from some uncomfortable objects: In the morning we left that dugout in a hurry as we had been sleeping with the most enormous aerial torpedoes.

This memorial situated inside the cemetery still bears shrapnel marks from the Second World War.

On returning to your vehicle look across the D937 where you should be able to see the ruins of Mont-St-Eloi Abbey in the distance.

After leaving the cemetery continue south for 2km along the D937 to reach the roundabout. Take the fourth exit and drive to the crossroads. Turn left onto the D49E1 for a further 2km until you see the **Leuregans Memorial** situated between two mature trees. Stop here.

You have just travelled along the former **Elbe Trench** which was used by the eight tanks from 12 Company, D Battalion, prior to the Canadian 2nd Division attack of 9 April 1917. Four were intended to support the Canadian 6 Brigade in capturing Hill 135, north of Thélus and the other four were to support the British 13 Brigade attack. In the event the tanks failed to make any material contribution to the attack.

The monument is dedicated to 19-year-old *Aspirant* **Austin Leuregans** who was serving in a company of older reservists of the 236th Regiment of Infantry when he was killed on 30 May 1915

The memorial dedicated to Aspirant Augustin Leuregans.

during the attack on the Labyrinth. Unveiled exactly eleven years later by *Général* Berthelot, it was financed from donations raised by his family and veterans of the French 53rd Division. On 30 May 1915 the 236th were ordered to take the Hambourg and Eulembourg Trenches in the field to your right. Leuregans apparently shouted out to his men – many of them over 40 years old: 'Surely, my old dads, you aren't going to let your child die alone?' His jibe achieved its desired effect and the attack went in but sadly it achieved little else for the loss of 460 men killed and wounded. A plaque on the monument records the division's fight for the Labyrinth: 'Here the 53e Division of the 20e Corps under the orders of *Général* Berthelot and the higher command of *Général* Balfourier fought during May and June 1915 for the conquest of the *Labyrinthe'*.

From the memorial continue along the D49E1 to the next crossroads. Turn left and in 500m you will reach the village centre of Neuville-St-Vaast. Park in the square opposite the *Mairie*.

Neuville-St-Vaast

The village was completely destroyed and rebuilt after the war, the Germans finally being driven out of the village on 9 June 1915. The central square where you are standing is named after the author **Roland Dorgelès** (1885–1973) who wrote *Les Croix de Bois*, which was turned into a film of the same name in 1932. He served in the 74th and 39th Infantry Regiments in the Argonne and Artois under his real name, Lecavalé. An information board on the corner of Rue du Carlin provides information about Roland Dorgelès together with a photograph of the centre of the village before the war. On the facade of the *Mairie* are a number of plaques relating to the fighting in the first two years of the war. The rebuilt church was opened in 1925 and some of the stained glass of the windows have a First World War theme, one of them depicting the Notre-Dame de Lorette Cemetery.

Outside the *Mairie* is a cluster of CWGC signposts directing you to Givenchy-en-Gohelle Canadian Cemetery, Givenchy Road Canadian Cemetery and Canadian Cemetery No. 2. Continue along the D55 to cross the A26 Autoroute and follow the signposts for the Preserved Trenches and the Visitor's Centre.

On arrival at the Canadian National Memorial Park turn right **A** into the Visitor's Interpretive Centre and park. There are toilets here. We suggest you use the plan of the Canadian National Park to navigate round the park and, as you did at Notre-Dame de Lorette, decide for yourself exactly what you wish to see. It would also be a good idea to familiarize yourself with **Route 2**, which will give you a perspective of the surrounding area. Further information and self-guided tour leaflets are available from the Visitor's Centre. Car parks are marked on the plan with **P**. Much of the 250-acre Canadian National Park is off-limits to the visitor; the site's rough terrain and large wooded area, combined with the numerous unexploded munitions that still litter the area, make the task of allowing the visitor to wander at will impractical. The very presence of grazing sheep to keep the grass trimmed highlights the impossibility of mowing the grassed areas by mechanical means.

A profusion of signposts outside the Mairie in Neuville-St-Vaast direct you towards the Canadian National Memorial Park.

The Canadian 4th Division Attack on 9 April 1917

The assault on Hill 145 by Major General David Watson's 4th Division – during which two Victoria Crosses were earned – began badly. The two

The new Visitor's Centre at Vimy.

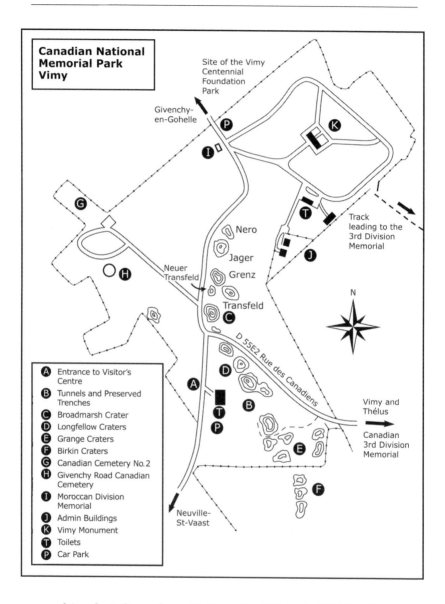

Canadian National Memorial Park Vimy

Site of the Vimy Centennial Foundation Park

Givenchy-en-Gohelle

Track leading to the 3rd Division Memorial

Nero

Jager

Neuer Transfeld

Grenz

Transfeld

N

D 55E2 Rue des Canadiens

Vimy and Thélus

Canadian 3rd Division Memorial

Neuville-St-Vaast

A Entrance to Visitor's Centre
B Tunnels and Preserved Trenches
C Broadmarsh Crater
D Longfellow Craters
E Grange Craters
F Birkin Craters
G Canadian Cemetery No. 2
H Givenchy Road Canadian Cemetery
I Moroccan Division Memorial
J Admin Buildings
K Vimy Monument
T Toilets
P Car Park

assaulting battalions from 11 Brigade, 87/ and 102/Battalions in particular, were ruthlessly machine-gunned by RIR 261 from **Batter Trench** as they emerged from the exits of **Tottenham Subway**, in what is now Canadian Cemetery No. 2. Half the battalion fell inside the first minute, jeopardizing the advance and putting the outcome of the entire attack in the balance. One of the hardest hit battalions in 12 Brigade was Lieutenant Colonel John Kirkaldy's 78th, which reported the loss of 20 officers and 774 other ranks. 4th Division's attack was the lynchpin of the entire Canadian attack on Vimy Ridge and, although Watson realized that *Oberst* Wilhem von Goerne, commanding this sector of the ridge, would stand firm in the face of a Canadian advance, the fierce German resistance obviously caught the Canadians by surprise. The assault quickly bogged down as scattered units of Canadians attempted to link up but it soon became clear to Watson that no organized advance was possible and the assault stuttered to a halt around noon. Calling 10 Brigade to mount an attack on 'The Pimple' and secure 11 Brigade's remaining objectives, a supporting attack from 85/Battalion finally managed to overwhelm the German defences on the west side of the hill. It was not until 10 April that Hill 145 fell completely into Canadian hands.

The Craters
After the British took over this sector from the French in 1916 the underground war intensified as tunnels were driven under the German lines and hundreds of tons of explosive fired. The craters give the visitor some idea of just how battered the ground had become by 9 April 1917. Behind the Visitor's Centre and in front of the preserved trenches are the Grange and Duffield Groups of craters. To the north is the Durand group which precedes a line of craters known as Longfellow, blown in March 1917 by the Germans. As you walk along the Chemin des Canadiens towards the Canadian Memorial a line of craters runs almost parallel to the road. **Broadmarsh Crater** – known by the Germans as *Schleswig Holstein* – which you can see just before the junction leading down to Canadian Cemetery No. 2 was where 19-year-old **Lieutenant Richard Jones** won the 25th Division's first Victoria Cross whilst fighting with 8/Loyal North Lancs on 21 May 1916. Under intense fire Jones kept his platoon together, shooting no less than fifteen Germans himself before a lack of ammunition forced the surviving nine men to retire. Jones' body was never recovered and his name is commemorated on the Arras Memorial. The crater remained in the hands of the Germans until 9 April 1917. North of the Broadmarsh Crater is another line of five craters which date from the French occupancy of the line prior to May 1916 and are individually named.

The Tunnels and Preserved Trenches ❸

Although the trenches appear artificial they were recreated by veterans who built up the original trench lines with concrete-filled sandbags between 1925 and 1927. The section of the **Grange Subway** that is now open to the public was constructed between November 1916 and March 1917 and is one of fourteen tunnels dug by the Canadian tunnelling companies in preparation for the assault on Vimy Ridge in April 1917. Connecting the Allied reserve line with the front line, these tunnels offered a great deal of protection to the advancing soldiers. The tunnel complexes not only incorporated railways, dressing stations, command posts and ammunition stores but also offered a secure shelter to thousands of troops. Check the times and availability of a visit to the Grange Tunnels with the Canadian student guides when you first arrive.

Canadian Cemetery No. 2 ❺

The cemetery was established by the Canadian Corps after the successful storming of Vimy Ridge on 9 April 1917 and to date there are 467 identified men from all 4 of the Canadian divisions buried here. The majority of the graves were, however, recovered from

The reconstructed trenches.

The exit from the Grange Subway.

surrounding battlefields and from isolated graves after the Armistice and of the nearly 3,000 burials only 821 are identified. Hence, the visitor will find graves from the first year of the war, casualties from the major battles of 1915, a few from 1916 and thirty-four casualties from 1918. As you enter the cemetery remember that this was ground where the advance on Hill 145 – where the Canadian Memorial now stands – by the Canadian 87/Battalion was halted on 9 April 1917. Even with the combined efforts of 75/, 85/ and 87/Battalions, Hill 145 had not been completely taken by the end of 9 April. Before dark, two companies of 85/Battalion managed to secure the western summit, but the hill's eastern slope remained in German hands. The next afternoon, 10 Brigade's 44/ and 50/Battalions finally captured the Hill. The 87/Battalion suffered 303 casualties on the opening day of the offensive, of which many are to be found in Plot I along with casualties from 75/Battalion. One of the youngest soldiers buried here is **Private Percival Moore** (10.C.38) who was just 16 years old when he was killed on 9 April whilst serving with 38/Battalion. On a clear day the visitor can enjoy views from the rear wall of the cemetery over the British support lines and the portal of Cabaret Rouge Cemetery may just be glimpsed in the distance.

Givenchy Road Canadian Cemetery Ⓗ

This battlefield cemetery contains 111 Canadians – one of whom is unidentified – all killed on 9 April 1917. The majority of the casualties are from 102/ and 54/Battalions which fought with the Canadian 4th Division. The eighty-nine casualties from these two battalions fell either during the attack on **Broadmarsh Crater** or during their exit from **Tottenham Subway**. If you stand by the entrance and look towards the A26 Autoroute you should be able to make out the remnants of the Canadian forward trenches. In support of the Canadian attack on 9 April, 172 Tunnelling Company had prepared a 20,000lb charge in and around Broadmarsh Crater but, as this was judged unnecessary to the Canadian advance, it was not detonated. It was a costly error that checked the advance of 87/Battalion. The 102/Battalion suffered 314 casualties on 9 April, of which 125 were killed or died of wounds and a further 189 were wounded. The visitor will also find casualties from the attack on Hill 145 in the form of men from 75/, 85/ and 87/Battalions. Another 16-year-old soldier lies in this cemetery, **Private Frank Ash** (A.22), who lied about his age when he enlisted in Vancouver and was killed during 54/Battalion's advance.

The Moroccan Division Memorial ⒤

Do spend a few minutes here as this memorial is the only one in the park that celebrates the French storming of Vimy Ridge in 1915. It should be remembered that if it had not been for the spilling of much French blood during the Battles of Artois and the subsequent capture of territory east of Souchez, it is unlikely that the Canadians would have successfully taken the ridge in 1917. The French advance in May 1915 would have taken them across the D937 which was some 2½km from the top of the ridge. The French success was so unexpected that the reserves were still at Mont-St-Eloi and Acq when they were ordered into action. For two days the division struggled under waves of strong German counter-attacks until on 11 May they were ordered to retire. You have already visited the Polish and Czech Memorials on the D937 where the men of the French Foreign Legion are commemorated. At the base of the memorial are a number of plaques commemorating the soldiers of fifty-two nations that made up the division.

The recently planted 4 acres of the **Vimy Foundation Centennial Park** is northwest of the nearby car park and was officially opened on 9 April 2017 in the presence of the then President of the French Republic, François Hollande, the Prince of Wales and the Duke of

The Moroccan Division Memorial.

Cambridge together with the Prime Minister of Canada, Justin Trudeau, and the Governor General of Canada, David Johnston. The planting of 100 trees was still in progress during the summer of 2017, the seedlings all being derived from the original Vimy oaks that were cultivated on his 'Vimy Oaks Farm' in Scarborough, Ontario, from acorns gathered on Vimy Ridge in 1917 by Lieutenant Leslie Miller.

Canadian Memorial to the Missing Ⓚ

Designed by Walter Allward, the monument, which stands on the top of Hill 145 and took eleven years to complete, commemorates the 11,285 Canadians who died in the war but have no known grave. It was unveiled in July 1936 in the presence of King Edward VIII. You will normally approach the memorial from the southwest, as the original 'front' faces northeast and overlooks the Douai Plain. The two towering pylons rest on a bed of 11,000 tons of concrete, reinforced with hundreds of tons of steel. The figures on the memorial were carved *in situ* by French stonemasons and on each side of the front walls at the base of the steps are figures known as the 'Breaking of the Sword' and 'Sympathy of the Canadians for the Helpless', whilst the two figures at the base of the steps at the rear of the monument represent male and female mourners. Other figures that embellish the twin pylons are those representing Truth, Knowledge, Peace and Justice. In 2005 the memorial was closed to visitors, opening again on 9 April 2007 after extensive renovation work.

To leave the site, drive south and at the junction follow signs for the D55E2 and Vimy along the wooded Route des Canadiens. After just over 1km a track on the left leads up to the 3rd Canadian Division Memorial.

The 3rd Canadian Division Memorial

Drive carefully as the turning between the trees is easy to miss. It is possible to park on the main road, between the trees or, failing that, there is a car park another 600m further along the road on the left. Walk along the track, bearing right after 75m to find the stone cross of the memorial near the site of the former Folie Farm. On 9 April 1917 the farm was one of the principal objectives of the Canadian 3rd Division and a great deal of heavy fighting took place in this area, the surrounding ground still bears the marks of shell holes and trenches. For the energetic amongst you it is possible to walk the 3km round trip through the forest from the Canadian Memorial Park.

Return to your vehicle and continue along the Route des Canadiens for another 1.17km to reach the junction with the N17. Turn right and continue for 400m to find the grass pathway on the right leading to Thélus Military Cemetery. There is parking here off the road.

The Canadian National Memorial.

The Canadian 3rd Division Memorial.

Thélus Military Cemetery
The oldest part of Thélus Military Cemetery is Plot II, which was made after the capture of Vimy Ridge. The remaining plots consist of burials made by fighting units from June 1917 to September 1918, except for those in Plot IV and part of Plot V, which were brought in from the surrounding battlefields after the Armistice. There are now nearly 300 casualties buried here – including 244 Canadians – of which over 30 are unidentified. This is very much a Canadian cemetery, so much so that in July 1921 Arthur Meighen, the then Canadian Prime Minister, dedicated the Cross of Sacrifice and spoke of 'the quiet of God's acre'. **Private Edson Callaghan** (II.C.1), aged 23, is one who rests in the serenity of 'God's acre'. He sailed from Halifax, Nova Scotia, in September 1916 with 148/Battalion and after a spell in hospital with bronchitis he was posted to 24/Battalion. He had spent just over seven months in France before his death on 9 April 1917. Also serving with the 2nd Canadian Division was 22-year-old **Lance Corporal Audrey Foster** (II.C.13) from White Rock, Nova Scotia. A book-keeper before he enlisted in December 1915, he was killed on 9 April serving with 25/Battalion. Another Nova Scotian was **Sergeant Major John MacDonald** (III.C.7) who was 25 years old when he was killed on 9 March 1918 with

185/Battalion. Enlisting in April 1916 in the 5th Canadian Division, he was killed near Avion whilst on a working party. In Plot V you will find eight men of 2/Middlesex, the battalion relieved the 1/4 Royal Scots in the trenches around Thélus in August 1918. **Second Lieutenant Fred Sharpe** (V.C.9) and **Private A. Simpson** (V.C.8) were the first to be killed on 3 August 1918. The enemy was using a large number of gas shells against the Thélus trenches in August and September and the remaining Middlesex casualties appear to have been the result of that action. Finally, **Private John Hobden's** remains probably lie amongst the unidentified soldiers. Killed on 9 April serving with 21/Battalion, Hobden's name is inscribed on the Vimy Memorial: the location of his grave in the cemetery was lost after the war and today he lies beneath a headstone bearing no name.

Leave the cemetery and continue the descent towards Thélus to reach a crossroads with traffic lights. To the left, along the road to Bailleul Sir Berthoult, is the Bois-Carre.

Bois-Carre British Cemetery and the 1st Canadian Division Memorial
The cemetery takes its name from the small wood of the same name that you can see further to the east. Begun by the 1st Canadian Division, it was enlarged after the Armistice with other burials from the surrounding battlefields. If you look over the wall at the rear of the cemetery you will be looking at the ground over which 1 Brigade of the 1st Canadian Division attacked on 9 April 1917. Unsurprisingly, the cemetery contains men from all four of the Canadian divisions together with those from British regiments and the RFC. Today there are over 500 casualties from the First World War and a small number of 1939–45 war casualties who are buried in Plot V. Nearly sixty burials remain unidentified and special memorials are erected to one soldier from the United Kingdom and one from Canada known to be buried amongst them. Other special memorials record the names of ten Canadian soldiers and three from the United Kingdom, buried in smaller cemeteries, whose graves were destroyed by shell fire. If you are seeking a headstone that personifies the tragedy of war, then look no further than that of pre-war Nova Scotian fisherman **Private Wilfred Nickerson** who served with 2 Company, Canadian War Graves Detachment (I.F.20). Nickerson had missed the war, only arriving in France on 24 May 1919 and died of multiple wounds on 4 June 1919, seven months after the Armistice, after picking at the nose cap of a shell with his knife: 'I've found some nice souvenirs' he

The Canadian 1st Division Memorial.

had told his friends, Privates Frank McKillop and Ernest Keizer. The shell exploded in his hand, the fragments fracturing his right femur and penetrating his heart.

The **1st Canadian Division Memorial** is another 370m further along the road on the right, but take care as there is limited parking. A grassed pathway on the right takes you across the field to the memorial – which was erected before Christmas 1917 – its position highlighting the open ground that the division had to cover on 9 April 1917 on the right flank of the Canadian attack.

Turn around and return along the D49 through Thélus to the crossroads where you will see the Canadian Field Artillery Memorial. Go straight on at the junction, on the D49 towards Neuville-St-Vaast, but first you may wish to take a closer look at the memorial. There is parking nearby, but take care as this can be a busy junction.

Canadian Field Artillery Memorial

The monument was erected here – at the Les Tilleuels crossroads – around the same time as the 1st Canadian Division Memorial just visited. One Library and Archives Canada photograph shows that it was certainly *in situ* – minus its cross – by January 1918 whilst another depicts the unveiling by Canadian Corps commander Sir Arthur Currie in February 1918. In his book, *The Great War As I saw It,* **George Scott** writes that the dedication service took place on 19 February that year. A contemporary photograph of the crossroads taken a year later shows the memorial but still depicts the concrete shelters that were in place around the crossroads and highlights the almost total devastation suffered by this area during the war.

Canadian Field Artillery Memorial.

From the Les Tilleuls crossroads the turning to Zivy Crater is a little under 1km along the D49. After crossing over the A26 Autoroute the access road is on the left where there is plenty of parking by the cemetery.

Zivy Crater

Zivy Crater was one of two mine craters which were used by the Canadian Corps in 1917 for the burial of bodies found on the Vimy battlefield. The second is the **Lichfield Crater**, which we visit in **Route 2**. The crater is essentially a mass grave containing fifty-three First World War burials, five of them unidentified. The names of the men buried here, all of whom died in April or May 1917, are inscribed on panels fixed to the boundary wall. The casualties are largely from the Canadian 1st and 2nd divisions.

After leaving Zivy Crater turn left to take the next minor road on the left after 500m, signposted Arras Road and Nine Elms Cemeteries. The road runs almost parallel with the British and German front lines of April 1917 and at the point where you meet the first sharp left-hand turn in the road, you cross the German front line. This is a recently improved road which runs parallel with the N17 for the last 450m before arriving at Arras Road Cemetery, where there is ample parking.

Zivy Crater Cemetery.

Arras Road Cemetery

The cemetery is situated behind the German front line of April 1917 and is roughly 450m from where the Canadian 1st Division attacked across the Lens Road. The division was commanded by 42-year-old **Major General Arthur Currie** who had Major General George Harper's 51st (Highland) Division on his southern flank. The 51st Division was on the left flank of the British Third Army assault and had a far more difficult role than their Canadian neighbours, a task that absorbed much of the punishment meant for the Canadians and left the Jocks victorious but badly mauled.

The original cemetery was begun by the Canadian 2 Brigade soon after 9 April 1917 and initially only seventy-one officers and men from 7/Battalion were buried here. You will find these men in Plot I behind the Cross of Sacrifice. After the Armistice the cemetery was greatly enlarged by the addition of 993 graves from the north and east of Arras. Today, there are over 1,000 casualties buried here.

The cemetery is probably best known as the last resting place of 30-year-old **Captain Arthur Kilby** (III.N.27), who was killed in action on 25 September 1915 serving with C Company, 2/South Staffords. Kilby was awarded the Victoria Cross for leading a charge along the towpath at La Bassée, during which he was wounded. Urging his men on to the German wire, he continued to fire at the Germans, despite having his foot blown off. Sadly, his efforts were to no avail: not one of his men entered the German defences. Along with Arthur Kilby, several more casualties from the first two years of the war are buried here. **Private Thomas Broom** (III.P.14) was attached to 1/Life Guards from 1/(King's) Dragoon Guards, and left Ludgershall in October 1914 for France. The Life Guards war diary tells us that the regiment was at Hooge on 2 November 1914 where they came under heavy shellfire. It was after this bombardment that Private Broom was listed as missing, presumed killed. It would appear likely that he was wounded and died later in captivity.

Irish born 35-year-old **Captain James Gaston** (II.N.38) was the medical officer attached to 4/Suffolks. His MC, which was gazetted in July 1917, remains on display in the Ballymoney Heritage Centre. Gaston died of wounds on 5 November 1918, six days before the Armistice. Two other men in the cemetery died of wounds days before the Armistice was declared, **Sergeant Douglas Harrison** (II.N.29) on 7 November and **Gunner Edward Williams** (III.P.2) on 8 November. Finally, find a moment to visit the grave of **Private Alfred Jefferies** (III.O.1) serving with 6/Somerset Light Infantry, who was executed on 1 November 1916 for desertion. His brother, Private Arthur Jefferies, was killed a week earlier and is commemorated on the Thiepval Memorial on the Somme.

> From the entrance to Arras Road Cemetery turn right and follow the road to Nine Elms Military Cemetery and the parking area.

Nine Elms Military Cemetery

Nine Elms was the name given to a group of trees 460m east of the Arras–Lens road, between Thélus and Roclincourt and this cemetery should not be confused with Nine Elms British Cemetery near Poperinge in Belgium. This cemetery was begun with the burial of eighty men of 14/Battalion Canadian Infantry in Plot I soon after the capture of Vimy Ridge. Three further burials were made in July 1918 but the remainder were brought in after the Armistice by the concentration of British and French graves from Vimy and Neuville-St-Vaast. There are now nearly 700 casualties buried here and of those almost 150 are unidentified. A special memorial is erected to one Canadian soldier, believed to be buried amongst them. Other special memorials record the names of forty-four soldiers from Canada and ten from the United Kingdom, buried in other cemeteries, whose graves were destroyed by shellfire. Four graves in Plot IV, identified as a whole, but not individually, are marked by headstones bearing the additional words: 'Buried near this spot'. The great majority of the British graves are from April 1917 whilst the French casualties are from the fighting in 1914 and 1915. Buried here is 20-year-old **Lieutenant Albert Hyde**, who was killed during 1/Royal West Kents advance on 9 April 1917. He was the only officer of the battalion killed that morning. If you look across the ground to the west you can see the area in which **Private William Milne** won his Victoria Cross as the Canadian 16/Battalion advanced towards the cemetery. Sadly, Milne was killed soon after silencing a second machine-gun position. His name is commemorated on the Canadian Memorial.

Retrace your route past Arras Road Cemetery and continue to drive parallel to the N17 towards Écurie. In just over 1km turn left – third exit – at the roundabout and continue underneath the N17 on the D60. Follow this road through Roclincourt, bearing right on the bend, to reach a mini roundabout. Turn right at the roundabout on to the Rue d'Arras and, after 180m, turn right again into the Voie des Croix. This narrow road leads directly to Roclincourt Military Cemetery where there is space to park.

Roclincourt Military Cemetery
On the opening day of the Arras offensive of 1917 the cemetery was less than a mile behind the British front line. The French troops who held this front before March 1916 made a military cemetery on the southwest side of the present CWGC cemetery; these graves were reinterred at La Targette after the Armistice. The British cemetery was begun by the 51st (Highland) and 34th divisions in April 1917 and contains numerous graves from 9 April 1917. It is sited almost on the divisional boundary between the 51st Division to the north and the 34th Division to the south, and continued to be used as a front-line cemetery until October 1918. After the Armistice, remains were brought into Plot IV, Row F. The cemetery now contains 916 casualties of the First World War, of which 32 are unidentified. There are also four German graves. During the war a wooden cross was erected in the cemetery by 22/Royal Fusiliers commemorating one officer and twenty-seven other ranks who were killed at Oppy (see **Route 4**) in April and May 1917. In 1920 it was removed, presumably by the IWGC, as it was then, and not replaced.

Lieutenant Colonel Edward Hermon (I.B.1), aged 38, who described the interior of his Nissen hut at Écoivres, is buried here. At 5.50am on 9 April 1917 he was killed as 24/ and 25/Northumberland Fusiliers (NF) attacked on the extreme left of the 34th Division sector, his final words to his adjutant were 'Go on!' Copies of his letters from July 1914 up until his death can be read in *For Love and Courage*. Serving in 25/NF during this attack was **Lance Corporal Thomas Bryan**, who was awarded the Victoria Cross for silencing a machine-gun post which had threatened to hold up the whole advance. Also serving in the same battalion were 34-year-old **Captain Thomas Blott** (II.A.11) and **Second Lieutenant Henry James** (II.A.27). Both men were killed on the same day as Edward Hermon.

Major General Cecil Nicholson's 34th Division attack on 9 April had as its objective the crest of the Point-du-Jour Ridge and although its task was somewhat easier than that of the 51st Division on its left, they were still initially lashed by the resistance of the 14th Bavarian Division. **Private John Herdman** serving with 26/Northumberland Fusiliers, had only just returned to the front line after being wounded on the Somme:

> You seemed to be in a mixture of exploding shells, clouds of dirt and bullets flying. When we got to the second or third line, I noticed blokes were going down all along our line, a single machine gun on our left was playing havoc with us. Then suddenly I felt a stinging blow on my left leg (again), and down I went. A bullet had gone clean through the shin, just above the ankle. Tom Bryant, our corporal, who had been advancing next to me, swore and ducked down. Then he went for the gun crew, he was mad but he knocked it out!

By the end of the day, as the division dug in along the bare, wind-swept crest of the Point-du-Jour, many felt that the losses of 1 July 1916 at La Boisselle – when the division's casualties had been the highest recorded that day – had been avenged.

Turn and retrace your route to the mini roundabout and turn right to pass the communal cemetery on the left. Continue for 1km until you come to a junction with a track on the right opposite a large white building. Turn down the track following the signpost for Bailleul Road West Cemetery. Drive slowly as in 170m – just after the slight left-hand bend – you will cross the German front line of April 1917. Continue to the cemetery where there is plenty of parking. The cemetery is accessed via a 20m grass track.

Bailleul Road West Cemetery

Situated in the middle of what was no-man's-land, the cemetery was begun by 12/Royal Scots in May 1917 and consists of two rows of graves, a small number of which remain unidentified. Eighty-four of the identified casualties are from the attack of 9 April 1917 and many of these are officers and men of 27 Brigade, 9th (Scottish) Division. Dundee-born 27-year-old **Second Lieutenant John Grant** (A.12) was serving with 11/Royal Scots and had been awarded the DCM in 1916 when a corporal in the Ceylon Planters' Rifle Corps. Described as one of the most unique British Commonwealth Regiments of the twentieth century, it seems likely that Grant served with this volunteer force in Gallipoli alongside the Australians and New Zealanders until he was commissioned. Serving with 6/KOSB were **Second Lieutenant Maurice Hillier** (A.7), who was only 19 years old when he was killed along with 30-year-old **Second Lieutenant Andrew Birrell**, who is buried in Tilloy British Cemetery. Another victim of 9 April was 27-year-old **Captain Thomas Martin** (B.1), who was the medical officer attached to 11/Royal Scots. Qualifying in 1912, he had been awarded the MC for his part in a trench raid on 21 March 1917 when he organized the return of casualties from the German line; but his luck ran out on 9 April when he was killed by

Bailleul Road West Cemetery.

a shell whilst attending the wounded. The five men from 12/King's Own Yorkshire Light Infantry (KOYLI) were all killed during early May 1917. Known as 'T'owd Twelfth', the battalion was raised by the West Yorkshire Coalowners Association and consisted largely of miners.

Directly opposite the cemetery, hidden amongst a large clump of trees, is the overgrown **Claude Mine Crater**. A little further down the track, on the same side as the cemetery is the **Clarence Mine Crater**. **Cuthbert Crater** has been filled in since 1961 but if you stand on the Arras side of Clarence and look at right angles into the fields the site of Cuthbert was some 125m away. The British front line crossed the track here at the Clarence Crater and the rear lips of all three craters were incorporated into the British front line after they were blown by the Germans on the evening of 4 June 1916 to assist a large-scale raid of some 500–600 men. The craters were duly christened with the three names taken from the popular music hall song of the time 'Cuthbert, Clarence and Claude', written by Arnold Blake in 1912.

Private Harry Drinkwater was in the trenches with 15/Royal Warwicks just a short distance away on the day the mines were blown and never forgot the 7 hours of unbridled fury of the action:

> Raper and Middleton went down … then [Philip] Jinks was hit … We were lying next to each other when a shell or rifle grenade fell close to his legs. We carried him into a shelter … but he was going fast. His leg had been practically blown off. Outside the air was livid as shrapnel was bursting … like flashes of lightning; come and gone in an instant, but coming with great rapidity with the attendant explosions and scattering of bullets. It was amongst this inferno, and with the knowledge that somewhere, not far away, the Germans were in our trenches and might be along any moment, that I had to try and render what aid was possible. Probably a hopeless case … and I could do little else than kneel by [Jinks'] side. He recognized me almost to the last moment and asked me not to leave him. I stayed with him to the end and saw him go west. I missed him very much: we had been great friends … The noise on the left of us was terrific whilst we on our part were keeping up a rapid fire with our rifles. The noise was intensified by the Germans springing a couple of mines in front of B Company. We were holding the right of the line and the Germans came in on the left. Of those that got into the trench only a few got out again, they were either bayonetted or bombed. At 11.00pm all was

quiet again; not a sound from a gun. Occasionally I saw from the German lines a lantern light guiding their men back in, at least those who had lost their bearings. Some never went back. We buried them later.

CWGC records indicate that sixty-three of Harry Drinkwater's comrades died that day and several others were taken prisoner.

On 21 March 1917 this sector of the line was held by 11/Royal Scots who were detailed to raid the enemy trenches opposite with two companies. This action was part of the continual raiding and counter-raiding that existed on both sides along the Western Front, designed to weaken morale and bring back intelligence as to the strength and designation of enemy forces. On this occasion it appears the Germans were quite aware of the intentions of their neighbours; not only was the attack delayed by a hostile aeroplane spotting the assembled men in Claude Crater, but there was a profusion of trench periscopes to be seen in the German lines. The Scots were subjected to a heavy barrage of mortar and shellfire even before they crossed no-man's-land, and when the attack finally went in at 3.30pm, accompanied by a heavy British barrage, the war diary tells us that they managed to breach the German first and second lines but were held up in *Schantekler Graben* – **Chanticler Trench** – by a stubborn resistance. The German account largely agrees with this but differs in the number of casualties sustained by the Royal Scots. The attack may have been delivered with great dash and enthusiasm but the cost in officers and men for the British was high:

> The English overran the first line in a rush and reached the second line. [By] 6.00pm the enemy had been thrown out of our lines in heavy close quarter combat by 6 *Kompanie* and parts of the *Sturm-Kompanie*, supported by parts of 8 and 11 *Kompanien*. A machine gun called *Kronprinz* received a special recommendation in the Division order of the day. During the hand-to-hand fighting *Leutnant* Haas and *Leutnant* Teichmann of 6 *Kompanie* were killed.

Casualties amongst the Royal Scots amounted to five officers killed or missing, two wounded and twenty-six other ranks killed and missing with some forty men wounded. The German account is quite clear that 'the English left seventy-six dead behind', a difference of forty-three between the two accounts. German casualties are recorded as seventeen dead, twenty-two wounded and thirteen missing. Both

Haas and Teichmann are buried, probably with a number of their comrades, in the **Neuville-St-Vaast German Cemetery**. Not content with allowing the Royal Scots to catch their breath, the Germans launched a counter-raid at 6.00pm on 22 March and stormed the lip of Claude Crater, capturing two Lewis guns and taking seven of the Royal Scots prisoner, reporting just three of their number wounded with no fatal losses.

Just under three weeks later 6/KOSB attacked the German line from here on the opening day of the Arras offensive. If you stand by the Clarence Crater and turn and face the direction of the cemetery, you will be looking at the German lines, the same view that the officers and men of 6/KOSB had on the morning of 9 April 1917. The battalion was commanded by **Lieutenant Colonel Gerald Smyth DSO**, a cousin of one of the authors who is described in the regimental history as 'a one-armed warrior of dauntless courage'. Stair Gillon describes the advance:

> The gigantic barrage fell sharp at 5.30am, and the 6th KOSB followed its pillar of smoke and fire. In a little over half an hour they had reached their objective, some 800 yards east of their point of start – a trench called *Obermayer*, just beyond which they pulled up in a sunken road, where they took prisoners in numbers, and let the 11th Royal Scots carry on the good work by taking the railway (Arras–Lens), which was the second objective, or Blue Line.

Later in the day 6/KOSB followed the advance to reach Point-du-Jour, where the memorial to the 9th (Scottish) Division now stands near Point-du-Jour Military Cemetery.

If you wish to visit the grave of **Issac Rosenberg** in Bailleul Road East Cemetery retrace your route back up the track, turn right at the junction onto the D60 then left on the D919 to find the cemetery on the right. **Second Lieutenant Eric Freear** of Harpenden, Hertfordshire, who was killed in the unsuccessful 4/Bedfords' reconnaissance at Gavrelle on 15 April 1917 (**see Route 5**), also lies there in grave I.K.6.

To return to Arras retrace your route back along the D919 towards St-Laurent-Blangy until you join the D950 Arras ring road.

Route 2

Vimy Ridge

A circular tour beginning at: Neuville-St-Vaast

Coordinates: 50°21′19.13″ N – 2°45′36.15″ E
Distance: 12.2km/7.6 miles
Suitable for: ⚲ †
Grade: Moderate (total ascent 140m)
Maps: Série Bleue 2406E – Arras

General description and context: The route covers ground occupied by the British in March 1916 and later by the Canadian 2nd, 3rd and 4th divisions during the April 1917 assaults. We begin in the centre of **Neuville-St-Vaast**, a village that sat on an area containing no less than eight underground caves or caverns which were used first by the Germans during the Battles of Artois and then by the Canadians, who maintained a large dressing station in an underground wine cellar in April 1917. From the *Mairie* we head down **Zouave Valley** to **Zouave Valley Cemetery** and the entrances to the former Canadian Subways to reach the outskirts of Souchez. Here we turn southeast to pass under the A26 Autoroute and visit the site of 'The Pimple' and the restored Canadian 44/Battalion Memorial. Returning down the track we pass **Givenchy-en-Gohelle Canadian Cemetery** following it past the **Crosbie Craters** to the Canadian Memorial Park. After leaving the park and the Canadian 3rd Division Memorial, a woodland track takes us first to Lichfield Crater Cemetery before returning to Neuville-St-Vaast.

Directions to start: Neuville-St-Vaast is best approached from the D937. Park ❶ opposite the *Mairie* in Place Roland Dorgelès (see **Route 1**).

Route description: The village was almost totally destroyed during the Battles of Artois which forced the military population underground. Canadian **Private Will Bird** from 42/Battalion recalled the state of his billets in Neuville-St-Vaast: 'Soldiers occupied the

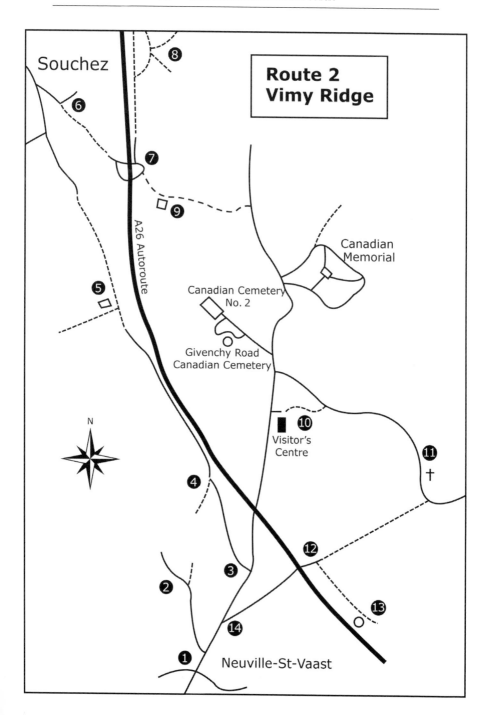

Route 2
Vimy Ridge

Souchez

Canadian Memorial

Canadian Cemetery No. 2

Givenchy Road Canadian Cemetery

A26 Autoroute

N

Visitor's Centre

Neuville-St-Vaast

The Mairie *at Neuville-St-Vaast.*

cellars. We were divided into groups and eleven of us were shunted into a cellar, in which timbers were holding shreds of wires. There had been bunks once. Rats ran into holes as we lit candles and then came boldly back and stared at us. It was a cold and wet smelling place.'

Keeping the *Mairie* on the right, continue along **Rue du Canada** in the direction of the Canadian Memorial Park. The road you are on runs almost parallel with the British front line of April 1917 which was some 1.2km to the east. After 100m you will come to a T-junction with Rue Verte on the left. Approximately 500m along this road the route forks and some 50m further along the left fork was the former entrance to the **Goodman Subway ❷**, which emerged some 850m southwest of the site of the 3rd Canadian Division Memorial, roughly halfway between the **Chassery Crater and the Albany Group** 170m to the north. The subway was one of thirteen that were dug by the Canadian tunnelling companies prior to their attack on 9 April 1917 and which, apart from Grange Subway, are either now closed to the public or slumber beneath the surface, concealed by the ravages of time.

Continue along Rue du Canada, passing the CWGC signpost directing you to Lichfield Crater Cemetery along **Rue de Vimy**, on

The Chemin d'Angres marks the beginning of the track running down Zouave Valley.

your right. We will be returning along this road towards the end of the tour after having visited Lichfield Crater Cemetery. As you pass the last few houses of the village you will reach the **Chemin d'Angres** on the left. Almost directly opposite is an unmetalled track which leads towards a water tower. If you walk along the track for about 130m you will see a tomb in the fields to your right. This is one of two former graves of French soldiers killed in the 1915 fighting that are still *in situ* on either side of the D55. The remains have long been removed and reinterred but the monuments remain.

Retrace your steps to the D55 and cross over on to the Chemin d'Angres ❸, from where you should be able to see the Lantern Tower of the Notre-Dame de Lorette Cemetery on the skyline. The track rises gently ahead of you and eventually runs parallel with the Autoroute on your right. It is worth pausing for a moment once you reach the crest of the rise to take in the view. To your left front you can see the full sweep of the Notre-Dame de Lorette spur with the Lantern Tower clearly visible on its summit. To your right, across the Autoroute, is Vimy Ridge and the Canadian Memorial Park. From this vantage point it becomes clear why the Notre-Dame de Lorette spur and Vimy Ridge were so strategically valuable to both sides in terms of observation and dominance of the enemy lines.

Continue. The route now descends into a valley – the **Vallée des Zouaves or Zouave Valley** – which took its name from the attack of May 1915 when the Morrocan Division stormed the heights of Vimy Ridge. **Quartermaster Sergeant Alexandre Robert**, serving with the 204th Infantry Regiment, was one of the first French units to arrive in the valley in September 1915 where they stumbled across macabre human detritus from a previous assault: 'Many skeletons, decomposed bodies, also litter the ground ... We identify them with shreds of clothing; there are Zouaves, Moroccan Infantry and Boche: a small pile of bones, of blackish dust around which the grass has grown more vigorously, that is all that remains of what was once a man.' Robert, in his diary account, writes of the **Talus des Zouaves**, which is the slope on the eastern side of the valley leading up towards Vimy Ridge, although the term is often used when referring to the valley itself. Six months later, in March 1916, **Major Frederick Mulqueen** arrived in the valley with 182 Tunnelling Company, RE and he recorded that he and his men were received by the French engineers who were both friendly and anxious to show the British the underground work then in progress: 'I was astounded to see a line of Zouave troops in their brilliant red pantaloons, lying where they had fallen in the attack ... Later I learnt the French had named the valley Zouave Valley after this famous regiment.'

The Subways
As you continue along the track until it turns left to run parallel with the A26, keep a sharp eye out at ground level as we locate the approximate positions of the other subways that were built to facilitate the Canadian assembly and advance of 9 April 1917. Some 225m after the bend you will cross the line of the **Grange Subway** as it ran left to right below the track beneath you. The entrance was some 50m off in the fields to your left. ❹ The Canadians began constructing the subways at the end of October 1916 to provide a more secure route from the rear communication trenches to the front line. Not all subways were designed as accommodation for the troops but all were larger in dimension than the tunnels and galleries driven during mine warfare. The Grange Subway, for example, was lit by electric light and incorporated headquarters dugouts, telephone exchanges and water points as well as dressing stations and accommodation for the troops. The Germans were certainly aware of what was taking place but could do little about it and some subways were completed just a matter of days before the assault.

You can visit the Grange when you arrive in the Canadian Memorial Park.

Continue parallel to the Autoroute for another 800m or so until you reach a track on the left. Some 50m due east of where you are standing – now beneath the Autoroute – was the entrance to the **Cavalier Subway** which was fed by a light railway. It had three exits which emerged in no-man's-land on the ground now roughly halfway down and straddling the access road to Givenchy Road Canadian Cemetery and Canadian Cemetery No. 2 in Vimy Memorial Park.

As the track descends into Zouave Valley it deviates slightly from the Autoroute and the surface deteriorates a little before you reach another obvious track on the left which leads, after 40m, to Zouave Valley Cemetery. The entrance to the **Tottenham Subway** was approximately 200m further up the track beyond the cemetery. Its two exits were in the vicinity of Canadian Cemetery No. 2. Both the Tottenham and Cavalier Subways were used during the Canadian raid on 1 March 1917, particularly for the evacuation of the wounded.

Zouave Valley Cemetery
The cemetery ❺ was begun in May 1916 and used until June 1917 and suffered badly from shellfire. After the Armistice the remains of forty-two soldiers (Plot I) were brought in from the battlefields

Zouave Valley Cemetery.

around Souchez. Today there are 178 casualties buried here of which 66 are unknown. From late 1916 the cemetery was almost solely used by the 4th Canadian Division and the visitor will find thirty-one casualties from the trench raid involving 75/Battalion on 1 March 1917. There are a number of casualties from the German assault of 21 May 1916 who were either killed on that day or died of wounds soon afterwards, although it is unlikely that 32-year-old **Sergeant Raymond Drew** (II.B.17) was one of them. He was killed on 24 May 1916 serving with 22/Royal Fusiliers, a day when the 47th Divisional Artillery fired over 32,000 rounds onto Vimy Ridge. Drew's father was a master at Eton College and Raymond was employed by the Bombay and Burma Trading Company before he enlisted in 1914.

The northern sector of the Canadian line in 1917 had to be approached through **Zouave Valley** through which ran a light railway delivering rations and supplies from Glasgow and Liverpool Dumps in the rear areas. Given the proximity of the railway that was used to transport wounded back to the main Aux Reitz Dressing Station via Neuville-St-Vaast, it does leave one to wonder just why this vulnerable burial ground was used at all after May 1916.

From the cemetery continue down the track and note how the ground rises up to the Autoroute on the other side of the hedge to the right. About 20m after the track bends slightly right **Vincent Street Trench** ran east up the hill. Its vestigial traces are still in the field. A little further on you will reach the location of the entrance to the **Vincent Subway**, running east alongside the line of Vincent Trench. Further along again you will see a small copse on the right with a patch of scrubland at its southern tip near the track. The two entrances to **Blue Bull Subway** (Blue Bell in some sources) were located a few metres up the bank on the tree line. Further down, where the track bears right then left in the form of a small kink, you will come to a collection of farm buildings. Look right across the open paddock and beyond the trees towards the Autoroute where the entrance to **Gobron Subway** was situated. Immediately after passing the buildings look right again and if the sun is in the right position you will clearly see the remnants of what was **Uhlan Alley Trench** snaking its way up the hillside towards the road, traced by a line of small trees, and the scene of a German attack to seize the British mine shafts at the northern extremity of Vimy Ridge (see below).

As you enter the outskirts of **Souchez** the valley rises steeply on your right, ignore the road on your left – Rue du 8 Mai 1945 – and continue along what has become Rue Victor Hugo until you reach

Zouave Valley looking towards Souchez.

a T-junction. Turn right ❻ onto **Rue du 19 Mars 1962**, following signs for Givenchy-en-Gohelle Canadian Cemetery, then right at the next T-junction to follow an unmetalled track which ascends above Zouave Valley. After some 400m – about halfway up the hill – the views over Zouave Valley open up to the west and if you look carefully you will see **Uhlan Alley** again, this time threading its way downhill. Continue and after passing under the Autoroute ❼ you will find yourself at a crossroads of tracks, ignore signs to Givenchy-en-Gohelle Canadian Cemetery, as we will be returning to this location later.

Turn left and continue uphill and as the track straightens note that you are now travelling virtually parallel to the Canadian front line of 9 April 1917, which was 50m or so to your right. This is the ground over which the German assault on the British lines was launched on 21 May 1916. Beyond the front line, 40m or so, were the **Momber** and **Love** craters, on which the German right flank hinged that day.

The German Attack of 21 May 1916
Much of the ground over which the fighting took place now lies under the Autoroute. The battle had its origins in the increasing intensity – and success – of mining operations that began after the British took

over this part of the line from the French in March 1916. A somewhat edgy situation was broken by **Major Momber** and 176 Tunnelling Company with the blowing of what became **New Cut Crater** near 'The Pimple' on 26 April, which in turn blew a German mine to create the extensive **Broadbridge Crater**. By way of retaliation the Germans blew another mine which formed the **Mildren Crater** and destroyed part of the British front line; 6/Londons suffering over eighty casualties in the explosion and subsequent bombardment. On 3 May 1916 four mines were fired by the British forming three large craters subsequently named **Momber, Love** and **Kennedy**. This period of retaliation continued further south with the blowing of several mines leaving what became the **Crosbie Craters** on 15 May. We pass the site of these later in the tour.

On 18 May 10/Cheshires of the 25th Division lost control of **Broadmarsh Crater**, now opposite the access road to Givenchy Road and Canadian No. 2 cemeteries in Vimy Memorial Park. Major Alexander Johnston, who had been appointed brigade major to 7 Brigade, 25th Division, in February 1916, was conducting Brigadier General Charles around the trenches when the news reached him:

We then heard to our disgust that 10/Cheshires had lost Broadmarsh Crater and the noise we had heard was the German bombers attacking and directing their fire … I went off at once to their HQ and finding their CO and 2nd in command had gone up to the trenches, I hurried on up to them as I was afraid they would be arranging a so-called bombing attack, which is quite useless and merely descends into both sides chucking bombs backwards and forwards.

The recapture of the crater was allocated to a company of 8/Loyal North Lancs, who, at 9.15pm on 19 May, crept out and, after a short fight, reoccupied it. By early evening on 20 May, however, the garrison holding the crater had been severely reduced in number and cut off by shellfire and to make matters worse the Germans had exploded another mine some 30yd to the south. The inevitable counter-attack followed on 21 May resulting in the award of the division's first Victoria Cross to 19-year-old **Lieutenant Richard Basil Brandram Jones**. Jones took up a position overlooking the ground between the two craters and kept the Germans at bay with rifle fire, 'counting them aloud as he did so to cheer his men'. He was killed in the act of throwing a bomb when the ammunition ran out. With his men reduced to flinging empty ammunition boxes and lumps of flint at the Germans the post was finally abandoned at 10.00pm that evening, leaving Richard Jones's body in the crater.

The 47th Division had taken over the Berthonval Sector, which included Zouave Valley two days before Jones's action. The divisional historian was unimpressed with the new line which appeared to have changed very little from the isolated posts and sketchy front line observed by Major Mulqueen two months previously:

> Our new piece of front was not a satisfactory inheritance. Lately the scene of destructive mining, it was in a bad state of disrepair. No wire covered the front or support lines; the front line consisted of disconnected posts, isolated by day; there were no shelters of any kind in the front system. Altogether it was a position ill-equipped to counteract the increasingly aggressive efforts of the enemy, who lost no chance in inflicting casualties on our unprotected troops.

It may well have been unsatisfactory but they hardly had time to become accustomed to their new trenches when the German artillery opened up on the afternoon of 21 May, demolishing an already precarious front line. By 3.40pm the bombardment intensified and in Zouave Valley, which you passed through earlier, a box barrage practically cut all communication with the front. German infantry from IR 163, RIRs 9 and 86, together with IR 5, attacked at 7.45pm with the weight of the attack falling on 7/ and 8/Londons, many of whom were taken prisoner whilst still in their dugouts. Reinforcements were hurriedly assembled in Zouave Valley as the German infantry crossed the old British line, stopping only to dig in when they had captured the British mine craters, some 300m from their old front line. British losses were heavy with the 47th Division recording 1,571 casualties, considerably more than the 637 recorded by 7 Brigade. The front line now consolidated along the line of the present day Autoroute before it swerved off southeast towards the site of Canadian Cemetery No. 2.

Continue up the track for another 275m. The site of the former **Kennedy Crater** was some 90m across to your right. In another 150m or so you will come to an obvious narrowing of the track. Stop here for a moment. Almost directly ahead of you were a line of craters consisting of New Cut, Mildren, Broadbridge and Football, where 6/Londons held the line prior to 3 May 1916:

> During six terrible days the battalion experienced a class of warfare that none wished to see again. Casualties had been

heavy: twenty-four had been killed, seventeen were missing and no less than fifty-one had been wounded; but when the battalion went out of the line on May 3rd, it was by no means downhearted, and was conscious of having acquitted itself well. Many will remember the march out, made notable by Sergeant Church, who played his violin as the troops trudged on.

The Football Crater was 300m straight on, along the track, and was the last in the series at the northern end of the ridge. Now look to your right, a farm track curves round to run right then left to follow a hedge line on its left. This path, which runs alongside an open field, leads to the restored **Canadian 44/Battalion Memorial** ❽ near to 'The Pimple', or *Gießler-Höhe* as it was known to the Germans. Before you take that track reflect on the fact that although Football Crater had been blown prior to their arrival, it calls to mind the service of the Footballer's Battalion – 17/Middlesex – which fought here in the summer of 1916. Boasting many highly skilled professional footballers from teams which are still some of the greatest names in English football today, 17/Middlesex arrived on 30 May 1916 just in time for the British to spring three mines in no-man's-land on 1 June as part of a plan to capture the far lips and advance the line.

The track to the 44/Battalion Memorial follows the line of the hedge.

The footballers attacked under heavy machine-gun fire but couldn't attain the far lip of the crater, instead clinging to the near rim. The attack subsided with 3 officers and 5 men killed and 39 wounded. The next few days were spent in strengthening the new line and on 3 June 1916 Joe 'Bubbles' Bailey – a pre-war Reading FC favourite – went up on top of the crater lip with his rifle and set himself up in a sniping position:

> I had a position that I could see all over the German lines to the Pimple only 150 yards away. I was also able to fire up their communication trench only 60 yards away. I stayed there exposed to the German lines for 4 hours and accounted for 2 or 3 which included a German officer with gold braid on his cap.

Bailey later went back up with Sergeant Wood and fixed in some steel plates for extra protection. From this safe position he was able to fire on the German snipers who had tried to do the same thing on the far side of the crater. He took his CO up to look at his positions and was congratulated for his work. Bailey went sick after cutting his hand on barbed wire in mid-June 1916 and missed the horrors of the Somme and Delville Wood. Later commissioned, he went on to become the most highly decorated officer of the Suffolk Regiment, receiving the DSO, MC and two bars and was Mentioned in Despatches. He resumed his playing career with Reading after the war and went down in the club's history, scoring its first ever Football League goal and its first hat-trick in 1920. One of the authors was honoured to be invited to speak at his induction into the Reading FC Hall of Fame in the spring of 2016. The craters in this area had been largely filled in by the mid-1970s prior to the construction of the Autoroute.

Now follow the track on the right and bear left to reach the 44/Canadian Battalion Memorial. The memorial stands on the German support line of April 1917. The original structure, which was demolished in 2005, was about 100m from the position of the memorial you can see today and stood on the edge of **Irish Crater** which was in the field to the left. Its demise was probably not helped by the removal of the cross and the panels on each of the four sides to Vimy Park in Winnipeg. However, at the suggestion of Jean-Marie Alexandre, the Mayor of Souchez, the new memorial has been positioned at the nearby junction of three tracks, not far from the summit of Hill 119, and was erected in time for the 90th anniversary of the Canadian attack in April 2007.

The restored 44/Battalion Memorial.

The area surrounding 'The Pimple' was finally taken by three battalions from 10 Brigade, 4th Canadian Division, on 12 April, an assault that was preceded by a short artillery bombardment and carried out in conditions of blowing snow and freezing temperatures. The 44/Battalion is credited with taking the actual hill with 50/ and 46/Battalions attacking a little further to the north through the wooded Bois de Givenchy – today's Bois de l'Abîme. With nothing left with which to defend the ridge, the remnants of the German 79th Division abandoned their trenches along with the village of Givenchy. **Sergeant McLeod**, who was advancing with 46/Battalion, recalled that 'The little fellow who loaded the rifle grenades for me had his head blown off. I was looking right at him and all of a sudden his head just vanished. I had bits of his brain scattered all over my tunic.'

From the monument take the track on the left – downhill – keeping the woodland on your right. The track curves left and after 100m you will see an access gate into the wood on the right. Enter and follow the dirt track until you reach a fence. Pass through and follow the track which, after a short distance, leads to a monument which looks like a grave on the left.

The memorial stone was erected after the war by the families of two young corporals of the French 413th Infantry Regiment – Louis

Hénri Pique (21) from Le Vésinet north of Versailles and Maurice Cabirolle (19) from Annet-sur-Marne, west of Meaux – who were found dead on 9 November 1915 after a heavy bombardment. Pique had been in Mexico when was war was declared and returned to France immediately to enlist in the 'class of 1914'.

Retrace your route, passing the 44/Battalion Memorial and returning down the track to the crosstracks by the Autoroute underpass which sits almost on the Canadian front line. Turn left at the crossroads and go uphill for 170m to find Givenchy-en-Gohelle Canadian Cemetery on your left. If you intend to visit this cemetery using a vehicle it is advisable to park at the crossroads as the track becomes extremely narrow near the cemetery entrance and turning is difficult.

Givenchy-en-Gohelle Canadian Cemetery

This part of the battlefield is where 12 Brigade, Canadian 4th Division, attacked on 9 April 1917 and the site of the cemetery ❾ is on the German front line. The brigade had already run into the stubborn resistance put up by the Bavarian IR 11 and 72/Battalion was becoming bogged down by a heavy machine-gun fire amongst

Givenchy-en-Gohelle Canadian Cemetery.

the flooded shell holes as the 11 Brigade attack on Hill 145 ran into trouble. The 38/Battalion fared little better as soldiers were trapped in the open and cut to pieces by Germans emerging from well-protected dugouts. It was along the track running past the cemetery towards the football pitch that **Captain Thain MacDowell** of 38/Battalion convinced a superior enemy force ensconced in a deep dugout to surrender despite the fact that only he and another man were challenging them. His award of the Victoria Cross was the first of two earned by soldiers serving with the 4th Canadian Division on Vimy Ridge. Of the 118 identified Canadian casualties

Captain Thain MacDowell VC.

in the cemetery 91 are from the action of 9 April, and the majority are from battalions of the 4th Division which include 27 men from 72/Battalion, 29 from 78/Battalion and 16 from 38/Battalion. Eight men were killed during the 1 March Trench Raid and were probably brought in after the Canadians secured the ridge. Of these, Cumberland-born 34-year-old **Lieutenant Charles Morris** (F.22) was serving with A Company, 72/Battalion, when he was reported missing in action and 21-year-old **Corporal Herbert Christmas** (B.1), from 73/Battalion, was another Englishman who emigrated from Colchester. He enlisted in Washington, Ontario, in November 1915. Finally, spare a moment for the two youngest soldiers buried here. **Private Joseph Furlotte** of New Brunswick (B.8) was 17 years old when he went missing on 9 April 1917 whilst serving with 42/Battalion. Furlotte was a descendent of the Mi'kmaq tribe, which made up the First Nations people indigenous to Canada's Atlantic Provinces. The other – even younger – soldier is 16-year-old **Private Edward John Nelson** from Sturgeon Valley in Saskatchewan (F.10). Nelson was also a First Nations descendant and was killed serving with 46/Battalion on 12 April, three days after Furlotte.

Leave the cemetery and continue along the track with open fields on your left and an expanse of private woodland on your right. It is amongst these trees that the **Crosbie Craters** still lie, and, for the inquisitive, a peer across the fence will reveal very uneven ground although the craters themselves are no longer visible due to the dense nature of the woodland. On 15 May 1916 units of 9/Loyal

The narrow track from Givenchy-en-Gohelle Canadian Cemetery passes the Crosbie Craters – in the trees on the right – before joining the D55.

North Lancs and 11/Lancashire Fusiliers were tasked with seizing two existing craters and occupying five more that were to be blown directly under the German lines. At 8.30pm the five mines were blown exactly on time and as soon as the lips of the craters had been secured, the working parties set to work to dig new communication trenches and consolidate the defences. The task was completed before dawn and by way of tribute to their commanding officer, who was temporarily in command of 74 Brigade, the Lancashire Fusiliers named the new craters the Crosbie Craters. Some of the dead from that operation can be found in Écoivres Military Cemetery. All was to be reversed on 21 May 1916 when the German assault pushed the British line back towards Zouave Valley.

The track continues past a football field on the left and curves left to arrive at a junction with the D55 after another 200m. Turn right here and in a short distance you will enter the **Canadian Memorial Park** with the **Moroccan Memorial** on your right and a car park and the Canadian Memorial on your left. If you have not already visited the park we suggest you refer to the plan of the Memorial Park in **Route 1**, along with the description of what took place here.

An aerial view of the Canadian National Memorial. The Moroccan Memorial and nearby car park can be seen top right.

Our route now takes us down towards the Visitor's Centre and just before the junction with the D55E2 you will see a large mine crater on the left. This is **Broadmarsh Crater** where Lieutenant Richard Jones earned his VC. It was also in this area that an armistice was arranged between the Canadians and the Germans of RIR 261 to enable both sides to recover their dead after the unsuccessful large-scale Canadian raid on 1 March 1917.

According to the war diary, the 54/Battalion attack went in with 15 officers and 390 other ranks at 5.40am supported by a discharge of gas but it was held up by strong barbed wire entanglements. Heavy machine-gun and rifle fire ripped into 54/Battalion killing the commanding officer, Lieutenant Colonel Arnold Kemball, along with Major Frederick Travers Lucas and many others. In total 54/Battalion lost 6 officers and 77 men killed and 7 officers and 126 wounded with 10 missing. The following night volunteers brought in several bodies from the ground where you are standing and to your right but many more were left out until an armistice was agreed with the Germans to clear no-man's-land on the 3rd. *Oberst* **Wilhem von Goerne**, the officer commanding RIR 261, was delighted with his regiment's performance in crushing the attack and although he could see the body of Major Lucas hanging on the wire, he could see no other 'English' dead from the front line:

I wanted to get a first-hand impression of what was supposed to be 'tremendous losses among the attacker', so in the early hours of the 2 March I entered no man's land under a cloak of a dense mist, accompanied by *Hauptmann* von Koppelow, the OC 12 *Kompanie* … before the wire entanglement lay dead Canadians in enormous amounts … the shell craters were full of bodies. When we were approaching the middle of no-man's-land and could barely see the outline of the first hostile trench, a shot rang out. *Hauptmann* von Koppelow raised his cane and shouted towards the English trench that they should stop the silly shooting. I said: 'Go ask the chap to come over'. *Hauptmann* von Koppelow had been raised in England until the day of his mobilisation. His mother was English and he still had an English accent. He even looked like an Englishman, which had lead more than once to him almost being arrested by overeager men assuming him to be English. At first nothing happened … Finally a steel helmet and, very slowly, a face became visible over the parapet; obviously the man did not trust the situation at all. But then he approached … We demanded to speak to his battalion or regimental CO and that he should ask him over … After about ten minutes an English major and two orderlies carrying rifles came over … I pointed out the many dead and certainly several wounded still among them. If he agreed we could negotiate to recover the dead. He agreed. We called several men from both sides to join us and gave strict orders not to shoot … Both parties obtained permission by telephone from their superior staffs. The artillery received orders to hold fire. In the meantime more officers and orderlies from both sides had gathered. I had sent for *Oberleutnant* von Trotha, *Hauptmann* Zickner, *Rittmeister* von Schwerin and several others. In particular *Hauptmann* Zickner and *Oberleutnant* von Trotha were speaking fluent English. Finally about ten Canadian and ten [RIR] 261 officers were standing together. We agreed to draw a line in the middle [of no-man's-land] to where the dead should be carried and taken from the enemy. As markers we used the many scaling ladders which had been carried for the attack and now lay around. This line had to be respected and no conversation was allowed among the men. Then the work began. Our men carried the dead on ladders up to the marked line and from there the Canadians took them back into their trenches. Soon all of no-man's-land looked like an anthill with busy people running back and forth carrying stretchers …

Finally we separated at 2.00pm and even shook hands. Soon afterwards an English officer appeared in front of our trench bringing the thanks of his divisional commander ... By 2.00pm about 600 – 800 dead must have been brought over ... In the meantime *Rittmeister* von Schwerin had taken advantage of the situation by scanning the field of fire and rearranging his machine guns.

Oberst von Goerne arranged another armistice for the next day but alas no further recovery of bodies was possible as the neighbouring Bavarians scuppered his plan.

Von Goerne's estimate of the number of dead was perhaps exaggerated; 54/Battalion's war diary records that 43 Canadian bodies were recovered including those of Lieutenant Colonel Kemball, Major Lucas and Captain Noel Tooker. RIR 261's losses had amounted to *Leutnant* Lieser – the regiment's first officer to die on the Western Front – in addition to fourteen men.

The funerals of Major Lucas, whose body von Goerne had seen on the wire, along with Lieutenant Colonel Kemball and Captain Tooker took place at Villers Station Cemetery, Villers-au-Bois at

The Canadian 3rd Division Memorial.

2.00pm on 4 March 1917 and were attended by Major General David Watson (commanding 4th Canadian Division) and several other senior officers (see **Route 1**).

Continue straight on along the D55 towards Neuville-St-Vaast and the Visitor's Centre. Our route now takes us along the track through the preserved trenches and craters ❿ to meet the D55E2 where a zebra crossing will take you across the road to the pathway on the opposite side.

Turn right on to the D55E – the Route des Canadiens – and after 750m you will find a track on your left which leads into the forest. ⓫ This will take you to the 3rd Canadian Division Memorial ⓫ (see **Route 1**). This is the area across which the 3rd Division, commanded by 43-year-old **Major General Louis Lipsett**, attacked on 9 April 1917. Much of the ground fought over by the 3rd Canadian Division is preserved within the boundary of the Memorial Park or in the Vimy National Forest, although it should be said that apart from the pathways through the forest, access to this ground is largely prohibited to the public.

By 11.00am on the morning of the attack, despite the 2nd Canadian Division encroaching into its right flank sector, Lipsett's division had swept through to the western edge of Bois de la Folie, the smaller Bois de Bonval and Count's Wood, the latter two of which overlooked Vimy village. Lipsett was killed in October 1918 whilst in command of the British 4th Division.

Continue for another 200m until you reach the sharp left-hand bend in the road. On the right you will see a track disappearing into the forest. Take this track, which becomes quite muddy in winter. One cannot fail to note the legacy of heavy shelling which still exists on either side of the track as it narrows to become a corridor running between fenced woodland to either side. Do not be tempted to explore in the prohibited areas as there is still unexploded ordnance in the woodland. A few metres beyond the point where the track curves left you will arrive roughly on the German front line – the Canadian front line was another 150m further on. At this point note that the former exits of Goodman Subway emerged in what is now woodland, some 300m off to your right. Crossing what was

Major General Louis Lipsett commanded the Canadian 3rd Division.

no-man's-land you will eventually emerge from the woodland at a sharp bend in the road at a junction of tracks **12** where a CWGC signpost directs you to Lichfield Crater Cemetery.

Lichfield Crater Cemetery
The ground on which the crater stands **13** was part of the Canadian 2nd Division sector and on 9 April 1917 the 24/Battalion advanced across the ground south of the cemetery towards Farbus Wood whilst to the north, 26/Battalion attacked towards Thélus. **Lichfield Subway** and its near neighbour, **Zivy Subway**, were used in the final assembly positions and were capable of sheltering entire infantry units as well as providing a base for battalion and brigade headquarters. Commanded by Major General Henry Burstall, the 2nd Division's performance on 9 April 1917 was almost flawless and by the end of the day it had taken all its objectives. The division was the only Canadian division to have tanks allocated to its attack, not that they played any part in the assault, but the sunken road in which they sheltered prior to the attack was called **Elbe Trench**, a road that we travel along in **Route 1**. Attached to the Canadian 2nd Division were the men of the British 13 Brigade who left their trenches 2 hours after the initial Canadian assault. By 9.00am 1/Royal West Kents had reached the Lille road, passing the tanks which had floundered in mud. At 9.29am an artillery barrage announced the second wave of attacks and the brigade advanced close to the barrage. **Coulot Wood**

Lichfield Crater Cemetery.

was entered and the Germans driven out before the battalion consolidated its line:

> The wood was held by A and B companies with platoon posts along the Brown Line and company reserves in the wood. Advanced posts were established on the road, in front and in touch with the 2/KOSB on the left. The reserve companies were posted in Thelus Trench.

Major General Henry Burstall commanded the Canadian 2nd Division.

British casualties numbered 287 with the Royal West Kents losing very nearly as many as the other 2 battalions combined.

Today there is a single headstone in Lichfield Crater marking the grave of **Private Alfred Stubbs** of 8/South Lancashire Regiment who was killed on 30 April 1916. The remaining seventy-one burials – fifteen remain unidentified – are all of men who died on the first two days of the Arras offensive in April 1917 and are commemorated on panels. The most famous of these is 25-year-old **Lance Sergeant Ellis Sifton**, who was shot dead on 9 April 1917 serving with the Canadian 18/Battalion whilst single-handedly attacking a machine gun that was holding up his company. His Victoria Cross, the only such award made to a man of the 2nd Division at Vimy, was gazetted in June 1917.

Lance Sergeant Ellis Sifton VC.

Retrace your route to the junction of tracks and turn left to cross the A26 Autoroute. Continue along Rue de Vimy to the junction **14** and turn left to return to your vehicle in Neuville-St-Vaast.

Route 3
Villers-au-Bois

A circular tour beginning at: the church in Villers-au-Bois

Coordinates: 50°22′21.46″ N – 2°40′06.72″ E
Distance: 9.1km/5.6 miles
Suitable for: 🚶 🚲
Grade: Moderate (total ascent 78m)
Maps: Série Bleue 2406O – Avesnes-le-Comte

General description and context: This route passes through some exceptionally fine countryside which does not readily spring to mind when thinking of the area fought over during the Battles of Arras. Villers-au-Bois was evacuated in 1914 and became the jumping off point for the French attacks on Carency in 1915. After the arrival of the British in 1916 the village was re-inhabited and various battalions established their headquarters in its buildings. The arrival of the Canadians saw a huge expansion with the establishment of the Canadian Corps reinforcement camp and numerous Canadian rest camps housing up to 10,000 men. At the junction of the D65 with the D58 the Canadian Third Division established its headquarters and there is a famous painting hanging in the National Gallery of Canada by **David Milne** (1882–1953) depicting a rest camp at Villers-au-Bois, although exactly which camp is unclear. The church appears to have survived much of the ravages of war, as the graffiti scratched into the exterior walls of the church by troops billeted here suggests it remained largely intact. Sanitation must have been improved by the 2/3 London Field Company running a motor and helical chain pump at a deep well in March 1916 near the church. Nova Scotian **Corporal William Bird**, who served with 42/Battalion CEF, had happy memories of Villers-au-Bois, which he revisited in 1931 and recalled was:

> a glimpse of heaven itself when you got there for a six-day spell and could sit beside a stove in the kitchen and toast yourself till you were thawed once more and dare look at your feet. It was,

and is, a third rate little place with dirty narrow winding streets, and huge walls jumping in front of you, and barns opening on the street, the whole an awful jumble without sanitation or system. But it was a perfect home to us when we came back from Vimy.

Directions to start: Villers-au-Bois can be approached from Souchez along the D58 or from Arras via Mont-St-Eloi on the D341.

Route description: The route begins at the church on Rue d'Eglise where there is parking. ❶ Note the lane opposite the church. A large French military cemetery was located in the field to the southeast of the lane before the British took over responsibility for the Arras front. Before you leave, examine the exterior walls of the church to find graffiti made by British and Canadian forces billeted in the village, some of which is contained within a glass-fronted display panel on the grass to the north of the building. For those who read French, there is also a useful information board with photographs of the village during the war years.

With the church behind you it is only a few metres down the Rue d'Eglise to the T-junction where you turn left along the D58 – Grande Rue. Pass the *Mairie* and continue to the T-Junction with the D65, marked by a CWGC signpost for Villers Station Cemetery. ❷ It was in the buildings on this corner that **Major General Louis Lipsett**

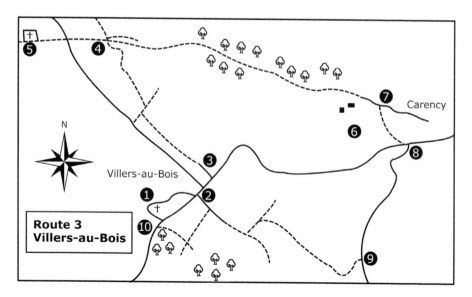

The church at Villers-au-Bois.

established the **Canadian 3rd Division Headquarters**. It is more than likely that the large building on the corner, as well as a number of the other nearby buildings, were occupied by the divisional staff. Continue along Grande Rue for another 130m until you come to **Rue Paquenette** on your left. ❸ Leave the main road here – noting the shell fragment impact marks on the old chalk walls of the farm on your right – and continue until the road becomes a farm track. This track was used before the war to access the former communal cemetery, which was on the right of the track some 200m further on and which, like the communal cemetery at Carency, was destroyed in the early fighting.

Go straight on to a junction of tracks, turn right and then almost immediately left, towards a line of trees ahead. The track continues and becomes a sunken lane – in which a light railway line ran linking many rear area villages in 1918 – before it finally curves to the left to join the former main railway line at a junction of tracks. ❹ Ahead of you a farm track leads north to the **Château de la Haie**, which is private property. Our route now takes us to the left, along the former railway line towards the D65 and **Villers Station Cemetery**. On reaching the main road, cross straight over and pass the former railway station building, to find the cemetery on the right. ❺ The

It is more than likely that the large building in the photograph, as well as a number of the other nearby buildings, were occupied by the 3rd Canadian Division staff.

cemetery and the nearby Château de la Haie have already been described in **Route 1**.

From the cemetery retrace your route to the D65. Cross the road carefully and stop. The area around you here would have been thick

Villers Station Cemetery.

with Canadian rest camps and training grounds, whilst the track you are on was once the bed of the single-gauge railway line running from Frévent to Lens which would have been in use continuously. After the arrival of the British and Canadian forces, the railway was used to bring the wounded back to the casualty clearing stations and to transport men and materials to the front. **Lieutenant Quentin Douglas**, serving with 2/3 London Field Company, recalled working on the railway in March 1916: 'The company worked on a light railway to run from Villers-au-Bois, through Carency station down the Souchez valley, through the southern outskirts of Souchez village and then southwards up Zouave Valley to the front.'

Continue to a junction of tracks **❹** and go straight across to descend gently for approximately 700m to where a track can be seen on the left, although at the time of writing the level of vegetation makes it difficult to see. This track leads to the Château de la Haie and after 1916 a railway halt called 'Dinkyville' was established here which allowed Canadian troops to access the rest camps situated around the chateau.

Continue downhill passing an electricity sub-station on the right, until the track breaks out from the trees onto a metalled surface with

The junction of tracks at the former railway line. To the left is Villers Station Cemetery whilst to the right the former railway descends into Carency.

The beginning of the track, which rises steeply uphill from the former railway line to join the D58.

private houses to right and left. If you look towards the top of the rise to the right ❻ you will see what look like the remains of dugouts or gun positions. Old French communication trenches seamed the hillsides to right and left here in 1915 leading to their front-line system. Later there were also divisional batteries positioned along the railway line at this point with ammunition being brought up by rail. Continue past the houses and round a bend until you reach a track on the right – almost opposite house number 46. Take this track ❼, which rises steeply uphill and from the bend follows the line of a French trench named '**Tocalen**', to join the D58. At the junction the trench went straight on cutting across the road and through the site of the old **Carency Communal Cemetery** which was located in the angle of the D58 and the **Rue de Huit Mai** which you will take in a moment. The cemetery was completely destroyed during the fighting in 1915.

Turn left at the junction and after 40m note Rue de Huit Mai on the right signposted Mont-St-Eloi. ❽ Turn right here but as you do note that the French front line prior to 9 May 1915 was some 40m further on along the main road to Carency with the German front line just 50m or so beyond that.

The road travels gently uphill – the French front line struck out to the southeast roughly along the line of the **Impasse de Feuchy** – before levelling out onto a plain affording all-round views of the surrounding country. On a clear day the towers of the ruined Mont-St-Eloi Abbey can be made out to your front left whilst the buildings of Arras may be seen a little further to the left. Villers-au-Bois is to the right.

About 500m after the last house turn right onto a track and stop. ❾ This is a good spot to look east and reflect that Vimy Ridge – visible on the horizon – is some 6km away as the shell flies. Lance Sergeant Frank Watts, of 15/London Regiment (Civil Service Rifles) was in the fields near here on the evening of Sunday, 21 May 1916; his battalion being rushed forward from Camblain l'Abbé on the day of the German attack on Vimy Ridge:

> we had just drawn our rations from the dixies when the company commander appeared at the door and said in a strange voice, 'Pack up immediately! Pack up immediately!' We swallowed our tea, put on our equipment and fell in outside. In half an hour the battalion was on the road, marching in the direction of the line. When we met the other companies it was obvious from the faces of officers and men that something serious was afoot. The old hands, I suppose, guessed what was coming, but to me it was all new. We came to the hamlet of Villers-au-Bois, and there rested in a field for perhaps an hour in the evening sunlight. The officers went away to receive orders. When they came back we took the road once more, my company leading the battalion. As we left the hamlet some Engineers ran across the road in front of us and climbed a bank on the side, apparently to get a better view of something. One of them shouted to his comrades as we passed, 'This way for the orchestra stalls!' Emerging from a belt of trees, we saw what they were looking at. Across a level stretch of country, two or three miles wide, we saw the Ridge. I do not suppose that it is much of a height as hills go, but it dominated the landscape at all times, and that evening it was as awful a sight as could be imagined. From end to end it was covered with a thick cloud of grey smoke, lit here and there by the twinkling flashes of shell-bursts. Seen across that peaceful-looking countryside it seemed unreal, fantastic, but there was no-one so new to warfare that he did not know what it meant.

Proceed through several bends until you reach a T-junction of tracks and turn left. From the junction the white buildings of Notre-Dame de Lorette can be seen to the right.

After 150m you will come to the junction with the Rue de Mont-St-Eloi/Rue de Villers. Turn right here and after 350m you will see an unmetalled track – the **Rue du Fay** – immediately after house No. 10 on the left. Take this track through fields to the next junction, turning right again onto **Chemin de la Chapelle**, which will take you back to Grande Rue. A right turn at the junction **⑩** followed almost immediately by a left will take you back to the church.

Route 4

Oppy Wood

A circular tour beginning at: the church in Oppy

Coordinates: 50°20′51.60″ N – 2°53′22.50″ E
Distance: 2.0 km/1.2 miles
Suitable for: ♦
Grade: Easy (total ascent 15m)
Maps: Série Bleue 2506O – Rouvroy/Vitry-en-Artois

General description and context: This is a short and very pleasant walk around Oppy Wood taking in the **Hull Pals** and **John Harrison VC memorials**. Oppy had been under German occupation since October 1914 and consequently had been strongly fortified with a formidable trench system – including many dugouts and machine-gun emplacements and protected by strong belts of barbed wire – running north and west of the wood; part of the Oppy–Mericourt–Vendin Line. In 1914 the layout of the village was entirely different from that which you see today and after the war it was designated a ruined village and entirely rebuilt. The village church, for example, stood some 150m further north and the stump of the road which is a continuation of the present-day Rue du Bois once ran north of what became known as the **Marion Mound** and on to the walled chateau and *Mairie* before joining the road to Bailleul-Sir-Berthoult. This through route vanished when the road system was realigned. Both the chateau and *Mairie* were destroyed by the British artillery.

Although the attack of 3 May by 92 and 93 Brigades is the most well known, there were three attacks made on Oppy in 1917, all of which were part of a much larger offensive. Gavrelle had been captured on 23 April by 189 and 190 Brigades of the RND (see **Route 5**) and the first attack on Oppy was five days later on 28 April. The attack involved 188 Brigade, RND, on the right, north of Gavrelle, the 1st Canadian Division at Arleux on the left and a very much under strength 2nd Division opposite Oppy Wood. Despite troops penetrating the German trench system and temporarily entering the fringe of Oppy village, the attack failed. After fierce fighting,

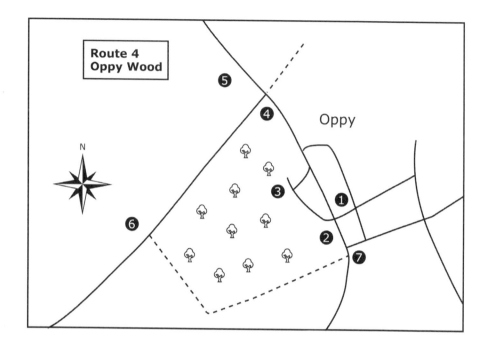

German counter-attacks drove the British out of the village and back to their start line. The only high point of the day being the Victoria Cross awarded to 27-year-old **Lance Corporal James Welch**, serving with 1/Royal Berkshire (99 Brigade), for his actions in the area west of the wood.

The British attack on Oppy on 3 May will always be remembered in Kingston-upon-Hull as a day of grief and loss; a day on which the city – and the East Yorkshire Regiment – lost more men than in any other battle. The attack involved the 31st Division and a much-depleted 2nd Division that 'had been reduced to a shadow of its former self' as a result of its attack just a few days earlier on 28 April. Facing the two British divisions were the experienced and rested troops of the 1st Guard Reserve Division and the 15th Reserve Division. With the 2nd Division on the left flank and 93 Brigade going in south of the wood, it fell to 92 Brigade to follow orders to fight its way through the wood and into Oppy. The units of the 31st Division formed up at 3.34am and even before they began their advance through the wood they were hit by a heavy German bombardment on their assembly positions. Whilst 93 Brigade made good progress, with some companies reaching their objective, it was a different story on the left flank. Here 92 Brigade found that the

Lc.-Cpl. J. WELCH.

Swallowfield Man Gains Coveted Honour.

THE greatest award for gallantry was on June 28th made to another man of Berkshire in the person of Lce.-Corpl. James Welch, of 1st Royal Berks Regt., son of Mrs. Welch, of Beech Wood Cottage, Swallowfield. This brought Berkshire's total of V.C.'s up to four, the three former recipients of Britain's greatest honour being Captain A. Turner, 1st Royal Berks Regiment, Thatcham (posthumous), Trooper Potts, Berkshire Yeomanry, of Reading, and Sergt. Mott, Border Regiment, of Abingdon.

Lce.-Corpl. Welch, who is 27 years of age, comes from a fighting stock, for he has two brothers and two brothers-in-law in the services, while many of his uncles have also been soldiers. His award was made

For most conspicuous bravery. On entering the enemy trench he killed one man after a severe hand-to-hand struggle. Armed only with an empty revolver, Lce.-Corpl. Welch then chased four of the enemy across the open and captured them single-handed.

He handled his machine-gun with the utmost fearlessness, and more than once went into the open fully exposed to heavy fire at short range, to search for and collect ammunition and spare parts in order to keep his guns in action, which he succeeded in doing for over five hours till wounded by a shell. He showed throughout the utmost valour and initiative.

A native of Stratfieldsaye, Mr. Welch, who displayed a most adventurous spirit as a boy, left school at an early age and for a short time was engaged in agricultural work. He was soon, however, fired with the martial traditions of his family, and joined the old Militia at the age of 17. He was than transferred to the Royal Berks Regiment and spent the greater part of seven years in India. Returning home soon after the outbreak of war, 1914, after a short preliminary training in England.

Wounded Five Times.

He has had a most exciting career overseas, having been wounded no less than five times. He fought at Neuve Chapelle, where he was wounded, at Fromelles, Loos, Deville Wood, Ovillers, La Boiselle, Hulloch, Beaumont Hamel and Oppy. The action in which he gained the V.C. was at Viny Ridge. The objective of B Company, a Lewis Gun section

of which Lce.-Corpl. Welch was in charge, was the position in front of Oppy Wood.

In describing the action Pte. Welch said the attack commenced at four o'clock in the morning. They went over the top under their own barrage. The distance to be covered was about 300 yards over open country. When the Huns commenced their first counter-attack he had to go to a high point and fire in order to keep them back. They were being strongly reinforced from their second line of trenches. He was firing on his own for upwards of an hour. There were six in the team, but four were killed or wounded in the taking of the first trench, leaving only Pte. Walker and himself. He left his position and fetched in four snipers by the threat of an empty revolver and handed them over, Pte. Walker meanwhile

LCE.CORPL. JAMES WELCH, V.C.

manning the gun. The Germans then launched a second counter-attack and entered the cap-search for ammunition and spare parts for his gun he did so several times under heavy fire. During one of these journeys Walker was either killed or wounded and he was then left to carry on alone. Finally, being hit by a piece of shell, he was compelled to give in and hand his gun over to a chum. When he left the enemy fire had quietened down. The Germans had failed for the third time in their attack and their casualties had been heavy.

The Berks captured three guns, bombs, mortars and other stores. The whole of the battalion did remarkably well, which is proved by the fact that 13 decorations were awarded. Hainge got a bar to his D.C.M., and Hilden, Plank and Rumble received the D.C.M. Capt. E. L. Jerwood, M.C., was wounded in one of the counter-attacks and his place was taken by Capt. Pocock. Sec. Lieut F. C. James was Welch's platoon officer. Welch took part in almost every kind of sport while out in India and carried off a number of trophies for running, cricketing, etc. He is also an expert marksman.

Corpl. Welch received his coveted award at the hands of the King at an open-air investiture in the front courtyard of Buckingham Palace on Saturday, July 21st, in full view of thousands of people. There were 24 V.C.'s to receive the decoration in person and eight were handed to near relatives of the winners. Co.-Sergt.-Major Edward Brooks, Oxford and Bucks L.I. (T.), of Highfield, Oxford, was amongst those honoured on this occasion. In presenting the decoration, His Majesty congratulated Lce.-Corpl. Welch and said he was proud to see that a member of the old brigade had won it.

To The Royal Berkshires.

They wear the halo of warfare's glory,
Erect of figure, and proud of face,
The Berkshires! heroes of Reading's story,
The noble type of a noble race.
A glint of steel in the golden morning,
The gleam of sunlight on burnished brass,
The Royal Berkshires, the street adorning—
The rank and file in their khaki pass.

The senses thrill with a keen emotion,
A sigh—a catch in the passing breath;
Must men like these, for a life's devotion,
Too often pay with a hero's death?
How many have known the days of slaughter,
The endless counting of comrades slain?
When red blood poured o'er the field like water,
When brave bones bleached on a distant plain.

In the foremost rank of the seething battle,
'Mid brave men dying, old comrades dead;
'Mid the cannon's crash, and the bay'nets' rattle,
The Royal Berkshires have fought and bled.
While women weep for their men who perish—
For battle's pain, and its awful loss—
In Berkshire, now, there are those who cherish
As legacy—the VICTORIA CROSS!

THISTLE ANDERSON.

Reading, June 28th, 1917.

The article that appeared in the Reading Mercury *in July 1917 recording the award of the VC to James Welch.*

felled trees provided both cover and strongpoints for the defenders and as the three battalions of the East Yorkshire Regiment became hopelessly mixed up in the darkness and swirling dust of battle, they were subjected to a murderous machine-gun fire. A number of 10/East Yorkshire Regiment (Hull Commercials) did, however, penetrate into Oppy before they were taken prisoner. Despite an act of outstanding bravery by **Second Lieutenant John 'Jack' Harrison**, which resulted in the award of a posthumous Victoria Cross, the East Yorkshires were driven out of the wood.

The attack on 28 June was along a 14-mile front from Gavrelle to Hulluch and was intended to simulate a threat to the cities of Lens in the First Army area and Lille in the Second Army area. Units involved at Oppy again included several Pals battalions of the 31st Division: 94 Brigade assigned to attack on the left and 15 Brigade (5th Division) on the right along a 2,100m front. Despite the German bombardment falling on the jumping-off trenches, the British troops advanced swiftly across no-man's-land behind a creeping barrage, before the German counter-barrage fell three minutes later. The German trenches were strongly held but the British arrived so quickly that few were able to resist and the wood was captured. Nevertheless, the shattered remains of Oppy village remained in German hands until 28 March 1918 when the German offensive codenamed Mars retook the wood and the village of Gavrelle to the south before it petered out in the face of well-sited and solid defences. The final battle for Oppy took place on 6 October 1918 when it was captured by 1/Sherwood Foresters.

Directions to start: Oppy is northeast of Arras and best approached by driving north from Gavrelle on the D33.

Route description: Park by the Church of St Nicholas ❶, which is now situated on the northern edge of the village green just a short walk from the impressive Hull City Memorial.

In the centre of the village green stands the French War Memorial which was unveiled in July 1927 and depicts a French soldier standing in front of a trench he has just captured. The observant will also see part of the commune citation awarding the Croix de Guerre to the village in 1920 for showing itself 'worthy and valiant in trials under enemy domination'. Was the partial defacing of this citation carried out when the village was once more under German occupation after 1940? Wreaths were laid at the memorial by the Mayor of Hull in October 1927 and at that time this space was overgrown with bushes through which numerous narrow pathways ran. Two corrugated army huts here served as a church-cum-school and blacksmith's shop.

Now walk across the road to the Hull Memorial ❷ which is on ground gifted by the Vicomte and Vicomtesse du Bouexic de la Driennays in memory of their son Pierre, an NCO in the 504th Tank Regiment who was killed at Goyencourt near Roye on 18 August 1918.

The church at Oppy.

The Hull City Memorial.

By the end of 1914 Hull had raised four battalions, each with over 1,000 men and 3 artillery batteries, a feat which, given the population of Hull at the time – some 290,000 souls – ranks as quite an achievement. The monument – conceived by Councillor Frank Finn in his mayoral year and designed by John Joseph Brownsword, the principal of Hull School of Art and a designer of Royal Crown Derby china – was the first to be erected on French soil by a Yorkshire city to commemorate all of its fallen, whether on land, at sea or in the air. It was unveiled in the presence of a large delegation in October 1927, including the Lord Mayor of Hull, Watson Boyes, Major Peter Robson, the Sherriff of Hull, the Mayor of Oppy, the Vicomtesse du Bouexic de la Driennays, representatives of the British and French armies and many French schoolchildren with Union flags and flowers. Even by 1927, although some families had returned to live in makeshift corrugated army huts, there were some Oppy residents who refused to enter the wood, believing it to be haunted by restless spirits.

From the memorial walk back down the road towards the church and take the next left – Rue du Bois. This road takes you up to and behind the rear of Oppy Wood. In the wood to the left on the crown of the right-hand bend was the rough location of the **Marion**

Mound, a feature which would have been visible in 1918 and which was described by the historian of 1/Sherwood Foresters as being in the eastern corner of the wood 'dominating all the country in its immediate neighbourhood, and forming the key to the holding of the wood'. A successful raid was carried out here by three platoons of C Company, 1/Sherwood Foresters under Second Lieutenant Greaves on 7 September 1918, during which the centre platoon captured eight prisoners of 17 RIR and a machine gun from the mound. The mound with its dugouts and machine-gun posts held out until the Foresters finally took the village on 6/7 October 1918.

Continue to a point where the road takes a sharp right turn into the Avenue du Bois. This was the point ❸ at which the pre-war road left the village and cut across the edge of the wood to emerge on the Bailleul-Sir-Berthoult road. Prior to 1914 the entrance to the chateau and *Mairie* was beyond the gate in the gardens to the left.

Continue round the bend to the T-junction and turn left – a German trench line to the left of the road followed the same route – and walk up the Arleux road for 200m to a crossroads. Stop here. This spot was known as **Crucifix Corner** ❹, and after the successful British attack on Cadorna Trench on 28 June 1917, the German line

Looking down the road from Crucifix Corner towards the John Harrison Memorial.

ran left of and parallel to the road, then cut back again a little further on before running north on the right of the road to Arleux. A line of wire facing north protecting the German 'Crucifix Trench' ran back east from here and connected with **Oppy Support Trench**. To give you an indication of the amount of ground captured on 28 June 1917, continue along the Arleux road for another 75m to where the ground on the left rises. This was the approximate position of **Oppy Post ❺**, marking the snout of the British front line, a post that remained *in situ* until the German assault of March 1918.

Return to Crucifix Corner and turn right to walk along the road towards the northwestern corner of the wood. Some 250m from Crucifix Corner is the point at which the former road, which passed the *Mairie* and chateau, joined the Bailleul-Sir-Berthoult road and formed a crossroads with a long-gone track that once ran to Willerval and crossed the D919 just south of Orchard Dump Cemetery. Continue to find the memorial to 26-year-old **Second Lieutenant John 'Jack' Harrison VC ❻** at the very northwestern corner of the wood. Jack Harrison had only recently heard of his award of the MC – gazetted in March 1917 – when his battalion – 11/East Yorkshires – began its advance from a position 170m from the western edge of the wood on 3 May 1917. Leading the men of 6 Platoon, B Company, Harrison and his men made three fruitless attempts to get through three belts of wire on the right. Finally, in the darkness and dust of battle, Harrison rushed a German machine-gun post firing from the southernmost angle of the wood and holding up his men, and in attempting to destroy it, lost his life. His posthumous Victoria Cross was gazetted in June 1917. His body was never recovered and he is commemorated amongst the thirteen Victoria Cross recipients on the Arras Memorial. There are two further memorials to John Harrison; one is at the Hull FC rugby league ground – a legendary Hull FC player, he scored 106 tries in 116 matches including a record 52 tries during the 1914/15 season, a record that stands to this day! The

The John Harrison Memorial.

other is at the Sutton War Memorial. An identical memorial to the one you see here at Oppy was stolen from Oppy Wood, in Orchard Park north of Hull in October 2017. Tragically, Harrison's 24-year-old son, also called **John Harrison**, was killed at Dunkirk, serving as a captain with 1/Duke of Wellington's in June 1940. He is buried at Dunkirk Town Cemetery.

Second Lieutenant John 'Jack' Harrison VC.

Before you turn left to follow the grass pathway alongside the wood, cast your eyes over the ground to the west towards Bailleul-Sir-Berthoult. The German front trench of the strongly fortified Oppy–Mericourt–Vendin Line crossed the road just 20m or so up ahead then ran off diagonally across the fields towards the cluster of pylons on the left in the distance. Turn left and take the path which skirts the western edge of the wood. As you continue, ponder for a moment on the attack of the East Yorkshires on 3 May which came in across the fields towards you from the right. **Private John Beeken**, serving with 11/East Yorkshires – John Harrison's battalion – painted a vivid picture of the assault for the *Hull Daily Mail*:

> Our shells were shrieking over us and bursting just in front. It was a creeping barrage advancing as we moved forward. The German shells were shrieking over us and bursting behind. Machine-gun fire swept the whole front. Different coloured very lights and rockets went up over the German line. Everything looked so weird in the fumes from the shells. Although we were only about 100 yards from Oppy Wood I couldn't see it, for a mist had descended.

The struggle to take the German first-line trenches meant the artillery barrage moved on ahead of the troops and in the darkness, exacerbated by dust and fumes from exploding shells and the broken stumps and foliage in the wood, the battalions lost direction and became scattered. Incredibly, at least one company did fight their way through into the village.

During the British attack of 28 June 1917, Oppy village and the chateau grounds were defended by 10 *Kompanie*, IR 73. *Gefreiter* Winter recalled that:

The Tommies suddenly appeared, pushing ahead, despite their own fire … It was straight forward close quarter fighting; section against section, man against man. An attempt by the company commander, *Leutnant* Goering, aided by a grenade launcher, to force his way forward into the open ground in the centre of the village and the walled chateau grounds failed at once … The company had to pull back to the edge of the village, but there it held on, a performance that was decisive in terms of how the day ended.

Continue alongside the wood following the track to the corner where it turns left again. Note how dense it is today, as it was in 1917, and recall that the British line had edged forward, almost halfway into the wood by November 1917. Look straight ahead: across the fields is Gavrelle with the Oppy water tower a little further left by the D33. The drains were in such a bad state after the war and usual water

The plaque dedicated to the Hull Pals in the church at Oppy.

supplies and wells so contaminated that building a water tower was a post-war priority. As you walk along its southern boundary look carefully into the wood and you will be able to make out shell holes amongst the undergrowth. The wood itself was cleared of the more obvious ordnance after the war but was not levelled before it was replanted.

Continue to where the track reaches the main road. ❼ The church is to your left. Before you leave the village, look inside the church to find a plaque dedicated to the men of Hull who died here on 3 May 1917.

Oppy Wood was immortalized by the artist **John Nash** in 1917 with his painting *Oppy Wood, 1917. Evening*. The shattered remains of the wood rise from an obliterated landscape above two infantrymen in a trench to the left of a dug-out entrance. One of them is on 'sentry go' on the fire step looking over the parapet into no-man's-land as shells burst in the distance. The painting hangs in the Imperial War Museum, London.

Oppy Wood, 1917. Evening *by John Nash which hangs in the Imperial War Museum, London.*

Route 5

Gavrelle

A circular tour beginning at: the church in Gavrelle

Coordinates: 50°19′49.86″ N – 2°53′09.82″ E
Distance: 11.9km/7.4 miles
Suitable for: 🚶 🚲
Grade: Moderate (total ascent 58m)
Maps: Série Bleue 2506O – Rouvroy/Vitry-en-Artois

General description and context: Captured by the Germans in early October 1914 after a brief but fierce struggle, during the next two years the village of Gavrelle – some 4 miles behind what became the front line – was woven tightly into their third-line defences along with Fampoux to the south and Oppy and Arleux-en-Gohelle to the north. It became a 'front-line' village after the successful British advance of 9 April 1917 had secured the high point – the Point-du-Jour – of the gentler southern extremity of the Vimy Ridge to the west and the village of Fampoux in the valley of the River Scarpe to the south and planning began to capture the Oppy–Mericourt–Vendin Line.

Gavrelle is perhaps most closely associated with the 63rd RND, which began to edge the front line closer to the village on 15 April 1917, captured it on 23 April – the opening day of the Second Battle of the Scarpe – and attacked again five days later in an attempt to push the line further east. The RND held on to the village in the face of determined German counter-attacks at a heavy cost. But many other units fought here including several of the northern Pals battalions of the 31st Division almost a year after their virtual destruction at Serre on the Somme on 1 July 1916. By the time they fought to north and south of Gavrelle in the Third Battle of the Scarpe in early May 1917, or again the following month, the battalions were a shadow of their former selves – Pals in name only – but there were still quite a few of the original members in their ranks.

The village was captured by the Germans again during their spring offensive of March 1918; the onslaught driving the British

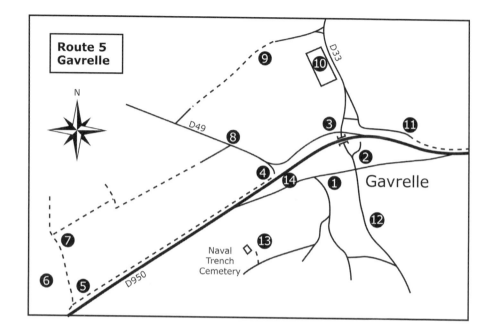

back towards the Point-du-Jour Ridge, to a position where the A26 Autoroute crosses the D950/N50 today, and it changed hands for the final time on 27 August 1918 when it was finally liberated by the 51st Highland Division.

Today the village is enclosed in a tight triangle of fast roads and a high-speed railway line. A little over a mile (2km) to east and west are the A1 and A26 Autoroutes with their junction located just southeast of the village centre, the line of the high-speed TGV shadowing the route of the A1. In the early 1980s work began on a new dual carriageway which completed the infrastructure triangle, looping across the fields and bypassing the village to the north. At a stroke the problems caused by heavy traffic thundering through the village along what was the busy N50 Route Nationale between Arras and Douai were alleviated but the resulting reconfiguration of the new road layout – blocking off several historic thoroughfares – effectively bisected the Gavrelle battlefield along a roughly southwest–northeast axis. Add to this the construction of large electricity stations in close proximity to the village and a profusion of pylons and the challenge for those seeking a coherent understanding – and calm contemplation – of the actions around Gavrelle becomes apparent.

We begin at the church in the centre of **Gavrelle** and head north, visiting a memorial to French soldiers killed during the struggle for the village in October 1914, before dipping under the dual carriageway to make a circuit of the gently undulating plain – part of what the British called the 'Plain of Douai' – so bitterly contested by the seamen and soldiers of the RND and several of the Pals battalions of the 31st Division during the two months of fighting from late April to late June 1917. The route takes in the locations of two Victoria Cross actions involving **Second Lieutenants Reginald Leonard Haine** and **Alfred Oliver Pollard** on 28/29 April 1917 before passing again beneath the dual carriageway to complete the tour with a short circuit of the village and the ground to the south. Here the Hood, Nelson, Drake and 2/Royal Marine Battalions of the RND suffered heavily in late April 1917 as did the Leeds Pals of 15/West Yorkshire Regiment in early May. It also covers the ground which saw heavy fighting during the German spring offensive in 1918 particularly that fought over by 1/16 (County of London) Battalion, The Queen's Westminster Rifles (16/Londons).

Gavrelle was finally liberated by the 51st Highland Division on 27 August 1918 during the Allied advance and after the war it was rebuilt with the aid of the people of Toulouse in the south of France. The village memorial reflects this debt with a dedication to St Germaine, the patron saint of Toulouse.

Directions to start: Gavrelle can be approached from Arras on the D950 or from the northwest along the D49 via Neuville-St-Vaast.

Route description: Park near the church. ❶ We recommend visiting the church and memorial at the end of the tour. With the French war memorial behind you continue to the crossroads, turning left onto the D33 – signposted Oppy, Vimy and Arras. After 75m turn right ❷ into the Impasse d'Oppy and go to the top of the cul-de-sac where you will find the memorial to the French 23e Régiment de Dragons – 23rd Regiment of Dragoons – on your left.

This relatively 'modern' memorial – erected in 1967 by the local commune in association with Le Souvenir Français and French veterans – stands on the site of a pre-war wayside chapel which was itself rebuilt after the war by the grief-stricken family of **Sous Lieutenant Paul Marie Joseph 'René' Grabias-Bagnéris**. Born in Montauban, 50km north of Toulouse, in February 1892, Grabias-Bagnéris was leading a reconnaissance patrol of the 5th Squadron of the 23rd Regiment of Dragoons on 2 October 1914 when it clashed

The church at Gavrelle with the French War Memorial in the foreground.

The monument to the French 23rd Regiment of Dragoons.

with units of the 1st Bavarian Reserve Division entrenched near the last remaining village windmill on the rising ground beyond the dual carriageway.

The Bavarians had occupied Douai on 1 October as the fighting spilled ever northward following the Battle of the Marne; both sides attempting to gain the 'open flank' advantage. The Bavarians had begun their advance from Brebières towards Gavrelle along the Route Nationale in the early morning fog at 7.00am (8.00am German time) on 2 October and by 10.00am the advance guard of four mixed battalions of 1 Bavarian Reserve Infantry Brigade under General von Kneußl had reached the outskirts of Gavrelle just as the fog began to lift. Spotted by French observers, the Bavarians came under heavy artillery fire and the advance guard rushed to take cover in the buildings of the village whilst others, caught in the open around the windmill, dug in. A machine gun was hauled up the mill stairs to fire out of a window just below the sail cap and the Germans steeled themselves for the French counter-attack. A tombstone-shaped plaque in front of the memorial tells the story of how René Grabias-Bagnéris died that day, fighting 'au Moulin de Gavrelle', according to his papers. The regimental war diary records that 33 men, including René Grabias-Bagnéris, disappeared but his remains, along with those of 11 others – 10 dragoons and 1 infantryman of the 306th Regiment killed near Oppy – were recovered and interred in the crypt of the chapel. Another plaque lists the names of the other men. Note the discrepancy between the dragoon named 'Bottereau' on the plaque and 'Battereau' on the back of the memorial. The man was Bottereau but his forename was Gustave not 'Gaston'. The infantryman was named Armand – not André – Clement.

It appears perplexing that a memorial should be sited at the end of a cul-de-sac until you realise that it is a casualty of the construction of the bypass. The road you are on was the original road to Oppy which was terminated here by the building of the dual carriageway you can see – and hear – up ahead. The chapel and crypt, built by the Grabias-Bagnéris family and dedicated to Notre-Dame-des-affligés – Our Lady of the Afflicted – was inaugurated on 2 November 1921 but fell into disrepair during the following four decades until the present monument was erected but prior to 1980 its location made perfect sense, standing at the crossroads of the main road to Oppy and the old road east to **Izel lès Equerchin**, close to where the action took place and on a spot where it would be seen by many passers-by. Today the monument and the plaques are tucked away in a glade at the end of a cul-de-sac whilst the graves of the men are casualties of the building of the new bypass; all now separated in perpetuity from the battlefield on which they fell.

Retrace your route to the main road and turn right to pass under the dual carriageway, then take the turning ❸ on the left – the D49 – signposted Bailleul-Sir-Berthoult, Vimy and Arras – almost immediately afterwards. Continue uphill and look right as the road flattens out just beyond the dual carriageway slip road. The line of a railway – some 250m away across the field from this point – which linked Fresnes les Montauban to Bailleul-Sir-Berthoult via the northeastern outskirts of Gavrelle, ran diagonally away from you northwest towards Bailleul-Sir-Berthoult. The railway served as the left-hand boundary of 190 Brigade of the 63rd RND for the attack on 23 April. Slightly over your right shoulder you will see a large electricity station surrounded by pylons. Beyond the electricity station you can make out **Oppy Wood**.

Continue along the D49 Gavrelle to Bailleul-Sir-Berthoult road, parallel to the dual carriageway. To your left you will see the spire of Gavrelle church on the other side of the bypass on what is the line of the Route Nationale. That road was the boundary between 190 Brigade, attacking directly towards you here, and the left flank of 189 Brigade which attacked the village itself across the bypass.

Continue to a right-hand bend with a track off to the left and a water tower behind trees on a raised bank a little further on the right. ❹ Take the track to the water tower and walk around to the rear edge of the plot beyond. This is a good place to view the northern sector of the battlefield fought over by 190 Brigade of the RND on 23 April 1917. You are now standing just behind what was the second or support line – **Filmy Trench** on British trench maps – of the German front-line system. This was the first objective – the 'blue line'– of 4/Bedfords of 190 Brigade. The front line – **Falter Trench** – was 80m or so to your left. Locate the nearest pylon with 'outstretched arms' then look northeast across the fields towards the mass of Oppy Wood following the track of the power lines to the left-hand edge of the electricity station. This approximates the line of the German second or support line as it ran to stand in front of Oppy Wood. It crossed the railway line some 450m away. 7/Royal Fusiliers assaulted **Falcon** and **Flabby** Trenches some 250m further into the field, about halfway between here and the line of the railway. Behind you and across the road the Bedfords also assaulted **Fatty Trench** as it ran across towards the dual carriageway.

4/Bedfords – the right assaulting battalion of 190 Brigade – and 7/Royal Fusiliers had orders to form a defensive flank for the RND assault by securing the vital higher ground to the north of Gavrelle around the windmill – 100m north of the site of the 23rd Dragoons memorial you have just visited – before bending the flank back along the line of the railway to the British front line about 1km further up the D49 towards Bailleul-Sir-Berthoult. On 23 April 1917 the men of **I Battalion** *Großherzoglich Mecklenburgisches Füsilier-Regiment* (Kaiser Wilhelm) 90 (FR 90) under *Hauptmann* **von Plessen**, had only recently arrived, relieving *Major* **Süderström's** II Battalion a day earlier. The men holding the trenches here had never served on the sector before and lacked intimate knowledge of the terrain and the three front-line companies had already been weakened due to casualties suffered under British artillery fire during their approach.

German accounts recall that the night of 22/23 April 1917 was:

> clear and cold, the sky full of stars under a dark blue sky, predicting another sunny spring day. The front was calm, only Very lights could be seen and the usual bursts of machine-gun and artillery fire could be heard [but] by dawn the silence was torn by roaring and flashing shell fire from both sides of the River Scarpe. '*Sie kommen*'.

The British creeping barrage opened up at 4.45am and the RND followed it in, one German account recording that 'the English … consisting of "*Marinesoldaten*" from the "*Marine-Division*", attacked in densely packed columns [astride] the Bailleul–Gavrelle and St Laurent–Gavrelle roads against the *Mecklenburger Füsiliere*'. A furious rifle and MG fire erupted from the *Füsiliere* in the fields in front of you, most of them mounting the parapet to fire point-blank into the ranks of 4/Bedfords and 7/Royal Fusiliers and temporarily halting their advance but successive waves coming through led to renewed momentum and the British overran the first-line trench held by the 2nd and 3rd Companies FR 90. 'The "naval men" granted little pardon,' according to the German account, 'few of the defenders were left alive, and [the British] established a defensive position covered by MG placed on the bodies of the fallen'. The English infantry then 'jumped off' again and managed to take the second line in a rush before veering left and right in an attempt to surround the few men of 1st Company and 1st *Maschinengewehr-Kompanie* (MGK) still holding the first line and cut off their retreat.

Leutnant **Billig** was with one machine-gun team nearby. Try to picture the scene in these fields over a century ago as he recounts his story of the fighting:

'*Herr Leutnant*, there they are', a *Füsilier* cries out and the silhouettes of men can be seen to the right [north] of the Bailleul road. We turn our MG around and fire burst after burst into the shadowy clusters. *Gefreiter* Krohn and I are hit by a shell fragment in the head, Krohn falls down soaked in blood, having lost consciousness. *Füsilier* Kiesbüge tries to save him by bandaging his terrible wound, but to no avail. Keep firing. The gun jams. One more burst. Again the gun fails: the cartridge belt is not fed well and tilts. One more try, and another … Suddenly the gun works smoothly. 'Over there', are they ours or English? Binoculars answer the question: *Engländer!* We lift the MG onto the parados to get a better view and field of fire. The MG fires perfectly and we pay full attention to the dense clusters of men. But 'Tommy' has learned too, he takes cover and advances by rushing forward in small groups under covering fire … making it difficult to find a proper target. Suddenly there is shouting to our right, Tommy has broken through and is advancing towards our flank. *Unteroffizier* Markus (2/90) gathers some men to prevent the attackers from mopping us up. Meanwhile the sun has risen and gives a clearer view: to our surprise our own artillery is shelling the ruins of Gavrelle behind us.

The Nelson Battalion had broken the German line and with The Hood in support were beginning their house-to-house fight through the village whilst The Drake advanced further south. *Leutnant* Billig was confused:

Has Tommy got through? Are we already behind his line? To our right the enemy has established a MG and fires into our flank, yet we can't locate the gun, so we make a 180 degree turn and strafe the groups of khaki-clad men entering Gavrelle, firing into their backs. But Gavrelle is under attack from the south too and we note a wave of English heading towards the village. So Tommy has broken through, no doubt. Well, it is our job to hold the position until the counter-attack begins to develop. Again we turn the gun, this time southward and fire one belt after another at a distance of 800 metres into the brown mass. But now Tommy … wants the hornet's nest in his rear eliminated. Infantry can be seen approaching from Gavrelle. Again we turn the MG and keep the attacker at bay for a short time, but again Tommy leapfrogs and gets closer, not only from the east but from the north too. We are surrounded on three sides: north, south and east. Only the western approaches are completely free of the foe. What a strange situation!

It is now [6.00am] and we begin to realise that there will be no way out; duty is the only thing that keeps us upright. We have fired 3,000 rounds in barely half-an-hour, only one-and-a-half muddy belts [of ammunition] is all that remains. No counter-thrust will bring relief, so we decide to call it a day. All remaining hand grenades are thrown at once, but they don't explode: God only knows what is going on … We strip the MG and wait for the enemy to take his revenge with the bayonet.

Although 189 Brigade got 'behind' the Germans and into Gavrelle and 4/Bedfords breached the line here, on the extreme left flank of the attack, 7/Royal Fusiliers had a torrid time suffering heavy casualties.

Retrace your route for 50m then turn right along the metalled track and follow it round until you are parallel with the dual carriageway. After 200m you will see the large anchor and brickwork of the RND Memorial across to your left on the other side of the bypass. A little further on, and looking again some 300m or so in the fields beyond the bypass, you will see a Cross of Sacrifice in line with a field edge.

The track runs alongside the dual carriageway.

This is **Naval Trench Cemetery**, which lies on the line of what was the old German front line of 23 April 1917 and became known on British maps as **Naval Trench** by the summer of 1917. The old German line north of the road was renamed **Marine Trench** and together they made up the Naval–Marine Line, the British second line of resistance which was hit hard by the Germans on 28 March 1918. We will visit both these locations later in the tour.

Continue for 300m and stop. The assembly trenches for the Nelson Battalion of the RND attack of 23 April 1917 cut across your path here but they were rudimentary. A few hours before the attack engineers laid two pegged lines of tape – 30m and 90m back down the track – along which the two leading waves would form up. The rear waves started from the assembly trench here, the attack going in towards Gavrelle on either side of the dual carriageway. The positions of the Drake Battalion were along this line to the south and those of The Hood another 250m or so along this track.

As you continue note how the bank to your left gradually increases in height as the dual carriageway begins its long, slow ascent passing under the A26 on its way up to and over the summit of the ridge at the Point-du-Jour directly ahead, before descending towards St-Laurent-Blangy on the other side. From this position you can appreciate why the British placed so much importance on capturing the high point of the **Point-du-Jour** ridge. From that vantage point in their third-line system – a concrete blockhouse 100m above sea level, on the site of a battered farmhouse at the summit crossroads – the Germans had dominated the British line northeast of Arras. This was the vital ground the British needed to secure observation over the plain of Douai to the east, towards Gavrelle and Oppy, and into the valley of the Scarpe to the south. The road at the summit marks the rough boundary between the sectors of the 9th (Scottish) Division – to the left of it as you look uphill – and the 34th Division to the right. The Point-du-Jour was the objective of the 9th Division's 27 Brigade under seasoned campaigner **Brigadier General Frank Maxwell VC**. In his official battle narrative recounting the events of 9 April, Maxwell tells us how it was men of his brigade who reached their objective: 'At the Point-du-Jour a party of 6th KOSB, filling a gap between our left and the 34th Division right, rushed a machine gun, destroyed the garrison and demolished its breakfast.'

After the war the 9th Division chose to erect its memorial near a stretch of preserved trench on the summit to mark its achievements, not just at Arras in 1917, but throughout its service on the Western Front between May 1915 and the end of the war. Unveiled on 9 April

1922 by **Major General Sir William Furse**, a former commander, the 30ft high cairn of Scottish stone used to be visible from your location here – squatting like a pepper pot on top of the ridge – as the architect had always intended, of course. Even when the Route Nationale was widened and 'dualized' in the 1980s the carriageways were routed either side of the memorial and vehicles had to manoeuvre carefully to gain access. Unfortunately, as the traffic increased in both volume and speed over the decades, vehicular access to the memorial became increasingly difficult and fraught with danger for the unwary. With the development of the land immediately to the north for the Arras Actiparc, it was relocated in 2006 a little further west on the Arras side of the ridge and adjacent to the Point-du-Jour Military Cemetery: a site which offered safer, albeit more circuitous, access via the village of Athies.

Some 40 to 100m or so off to your right and parallel to the track here, a German communication trench – *Gavreller Weg* – had zig-zagged its way from the line in front of Gavrelle towards the Point-du-Jour ridge prior to 9 April 1917. This trench was renamed **Thames Alley** after the capture of the village and became a main artery for feeding the British line east of Gavrelle.

Continue but pause at a point some 300m from the overpass which takes the A26 over the dual carriageway. A lay-by on the other side of the bypass, directly opposite, is now home to a pink granite demarcation stone which marks the furthest point of the German advance on this sector during their offensive of 1918. The Germans reoccupied the village and all the ground gained by the British in the spring and summer of 1917 but were halted before they could get on to the Point-du-Jour ridge proper.

Turn right just before the flyover to take the farm track ❺ and stop. In 1917 the track intersected the Route Nationale at a crossroads here. The crossroads was the site of what was known as **Lonely House** and a cemetery was begun here after 23 April 1917 which eventually contained the graves of twenty-five sailors, soldiers and Royal Marine Light Infantry (RMLI) killed between April and July 1917. Their remains were exhumed after the war and re-interred in Point-du-Jour Military Cemetery.

Continue up the track for 200m and stop between the two pylons. Look directly across the fields to the west – along a line parallel with the line of the A26 – to a clump of trees and rough scrub. This marks the site of a pre-April 1917 German concrete field gun emplacement in the lee of the ridge. ❻ Now much overgrown, access is possible by following the field edge and hugging the fence line on the bank of the Autoroute, until striking another rough track and turning right to reach the gun emplacement.

The track you are now on was specifically named as the basis for construction of the support line in defence-scheme documents drawn up by the 63rd RND on taking over responsibility for this sector from the 34th Division on the night of 14/15 April 1917. By early 1918 the British had responded to the German doctrine of 'elastic' defence and had adopted their own scheme of defence in depth, consisting of an 'outpost' line east of Gavrelle, a second line of resistance along the Naval–Marine Line you passed through earlier and a third line of resistance roughly following the track here. This became the **Bailleul–Willerval–Chaudier–Hirondelle Line**. Studding the trench line were a series of carefully sited, well-wired strongpoints or field redoubts with all-round fields of fire. You are now in the heart of one of them – **Ditch Post** – named after a ditch which ran off at right angles into the field to the right roughly following the direction of the electricity lines. The last and main line of resistance was the key tactical feature of the Point-du-Jour ridge off to the west.

Continue along the track, uphill, shadowing what became known as **Kilkerran Support Trench** dug in the fields to the right. As you do so reflect on the fact that the opening bombardment of the German onslaught of 28 March 1918 rained high-explosive and gas shells down onto this area forcing the troops to keep their box respirators on for 3 hours. Ditch Post and the trenches to the south 'were very badly knocked about'. When the German attack finally went in continuous 'lines of men shoulder to shoulder' drove about 160 survivors of 16/Londons of the 56th Division back from their positions on the outpost line at Towy Post, south of the village cemetery, to this spot by 11.00am. Here they joined men of 1/2 Londons (Royal Fusiliers) holding the line and sixty survivors of 1/5 Londons (London Rifle Brigade) forced from their posts north of Gavrelle. The line here was ordered to be 'held at all costs'. And so it was. A spirited, tactical fighting withdrawal was transformed into a successful stand and the German surge was finally checked in spite of repeated attempts to dislodge the Londoners with the support of ground-strafing aircraft. The line stabilized at about 6.00pm that evening – hence the location of the demarcation stone passed earlier – and maps from April 1918 clearly mark this track as being on the 'British Front Line'. It was only advanced a short distance to the east prior to the final Advance to Victory in August 1918.

Continue along the track which leads to Bailleul-Sir-Berthoult. As it becomes slightly sunken you will see another track on the right. ❼

Another of the British third-line strongpoints – **Bailleul Post** – was 350m further on towards the village but you will turn right here. You are now heading towards the electricity station and the track is on the line of 190 Brigade's advance on 23 April 1917. Up ahead and slightly to the right you will see the water tower on the D49, visited earlier, which marks the position of the German line that day.

Follow the track through two right-angled bends then stop after 150m. The fields to the left of the track here were the scene of a very bloody but often overlooked action the day after the 63rd RND arrived on the sector on 14 April 1917. Look around and consider the ground here. In his history of the RND, **Douglas Jerrold**, who had served with the **Hawke Battalion** during the war, noted that the new positions were:

> unenviable ... the new front line lay on the forward slope of the [Point-du-Jour ridge] looking down into the plain of Gavrelle ... From the crest of the hill to the enemy's line ... was a perfectly open belt of country more than 3,500 yards in depth ... our front line [and] communications were at the mercy of an observant enemy.

Imagine being in the line on unfamiliar ground here during that raw spring of 1917, the weather being 'bitterly cold, snow alternated with sleet'.

The outposts of 189 Brigade were within 'striking distance' of the German trenches on the right and so the first task of **Brigadier General Finch** was to push his 190 Brigade outposts forward in the fields to the north here to conform with 189 Brigade's line. The task of this 'reconnaissance' fell to the men of 10/Royal Dublin Fusiliers, with 4/Bedfords, on their left, who set out to advance 1,000yd on the morning of 15 April 1917 without any artillery preparation, in what Jerrold described as 'an audacious attempt to advance our line in broad daylight across ground commanded by the enemy'. Both battalions were severely punished. The 10/Dublin Fusiliers war diary entry is brief: 'Owing to the very heavy hostile artillery and machine gun fire, the attempt was unsuccessful. Our casualties were estimated at about 5 Officers and 80 other ranks.' 1/Honourable Artillery Company (1/HAC) was in the same brigade as the Dublins and Bedfords. Its first task on this new sector was grim: 'The battalion spent all the forenoon clearing the battlefield and burying the dead.'

CWGC records indicate that fourteen men of 10/Royal Dublin Fusiliers were killed; six of whom, including Bombay-born **Private**

James O'Connor, now lie in Orchard Dump Cemetery, Arleux. The bodies of the rest, including **Second Lieutenant George Allgood**, were never recovered or identified and their names are on the Arras Memorial to the Missing.

The Bedfords' casualty figures – five officers and fifty-five men – were not as heavy on paper but they actually fared worse: two officers – **Second Lieutenants Eric Freear** and **Ambrose Marshall** (Hertfordshire Regiment, attached to the Bedfords) – were killed whilst **Lieutenant**

Second Lieutenant George Allgood.

George Wray, **Second Lieutenant Jessel Anidjar Romain** and **Second Lieutenant Mogridge** were wounded. Eighteen other ranks were killed of whom thirteen have no known grave.

Proceed to the end of the track and the junction with the D49. Stop here. ❽ The German line of 15 April 1917 crossed the D49 at right angles about 225m to your right. Further probing by 1/HAC and 7/Royal Fusiliers during the following two nights – including a

The view along the track towards the junction with the D33. The water tower is next to the D33 road at the entrance to Oppy.

patrol led by Second Lieutenant Alfred Oliver Pollard MC of 1/HAC on 16 April – found the German wire in three belts and the line to be strongly held. Nevertheless, they persevered in edging forward and finally dug in 300m from the German wire; a point some 200m along the D49 to your left.

Directly ahead and to the left is Oppy Wood, marked by the white water tower, and beyond, if visibility is good, you can make out several slag heaps of the Douai coalfield.

Turn left along the D49 then take the metalled track on the right after 400m. Look left as the track skirts the southern fringes of the unspectacular rising ground to the north. This is the highest point on the plain here – known as Hill 80 – and in March 1918 its western slope was the location of the Bailleul East strongpoint in the British third line. After another 260m you will strike the line of the railway which came in across the fields diagonally towards you from the area to the right of the electricity station, before it crossed the track and curved northeast to run around Hill 80. This should have become the protecting left flank after the 23 April 1917 attack,

Look into the fields about 350m to your right – at about 1 o'clock – towards a group of pylons and locate another large pylon with 'outstretched arms'. This approximates the site of what was the German front line and wire entanglement. As the first two waves – A and D Companies – of 7/Royal Fusiliers reached the German wire here a little after 4.45am on 23 April 1917 they found it intact. The leading Fusiliers bunched to get through what appeared to be a single narrow lane and the Germans rained bombs on them from the front line. Those who got through lost direction. By 5.20am **Second Lieutenant Taylor**, commanding D Company, reported that 'My company has taken enemy 2nd line and have taken about 23 prisoners and one MG. Our casualties are about 40%. I am in touch with the Bedfords on my right and 2nd Div on my left. A Company have lost all their officers and I have taken command.'

By 8.30am German machine-gunners and snipers were still holding their first and second lines just south of the railway near the 'outstretched arms' pylon and were exacting a heavy toll on the Fusiliers. By that time 23-year-old **Captain William George Gush** in command of B Company had been killed. Originally from Seaton in Devon, after the war William Gush's architect father George placed a memorial tablet to his son on the east wall of the Seaton United Reformed Church, a church which George Gush had designed in 1894: 'In loving memory of William George Gush, Captain 7th Battalion Royal Fusiliers, only son of George and Emily Hannah

Gush, and grandson of the late Revd. W Phillips, killed in action at Gavrelle, France on the 23rd April 1917, aged 23 years'.

D Company was down to about twenty-five men by 9.30am, held up and unable to advance beyond that spot. At 9.40am **Second Lieutenant Greenwood** of D Company reported that 'We are consolidating our present position and have a party of about 40 consisting of all companies of the Fusiliers still being held up by machine guns.'

Now the Germans began their counter-attack, filtering men across the railway and down Falcon and Flabby Trenches to bomb their way southwest whilst a small party of just twenty-two Fusiliers tried to stem the tide and bomb them back. The fighting around the site of that pylon went on all afternoon but the Fusiliers could not reach the railway and by 5.45pm had to content themselves with establishing bomb blocks 25–30m from the railway – a spot between the two pylons nearest you – and digging a trench back to the original British front line until they were relieved in the early hours of 24 April. The Fusiliers' war diarist returned casualties amounting to 353, including 4 officers and 36 men killed and 84 men missing. CWGC records today indicate that 4 officers, 13 NCOs and 77 men were killed on 23/24 April 1917, the vast majority have no known grave.

One of the men killed somewhere in the fields near the pylons was 23-year-old **Captain Basil Granville** who had been in command of C Company in the 7/Royal Fusiliers' fourth wave. By the time he went into action at Gavrelle, Basil had already led an interesting life. He had been born Basil Hosken in Helston, Cornwall to Charlotte and Charles Hosken, a sometime solicitor, failed businessman, author and 'rogue' who went on to become a fraudster and serial bigamist with many aliases. Charles Hosken had adopted the pen name 'Granville' around 1898 when Basil was 4 and deserted his mother in about 1908. He went on to be jailed for fraud and bigamy in 1913. Basil was in Brussels with his forsaken mother when war broke out and witnessed the German occupation before fleeing through the lines to escape to England. He joined the Public Schools and Universities Corps and was commissioned in May 1915. Wounded on the Somme, he was raised to an acting captaincy six weeks before the battle on 23 April 1917 and was killed in the German front line at about 9.30am.

In a letter to Basil's father, his commanding officer, **Lieutenant Colonel Rawdon Hesketh**, wrote: 'The battalion, with many others, attacked the enemy's position in the early morning of the 23rd. Though there was a good deal of resistance we gained our objective and your son was gallantly leading his men when he was hit in the head by a sniper and killed instantaneously.'

Despite his dubious past, Basil's father obviously mourned for his lost son. He was inspired to write a poem 'For Parents of the Slain' which was published in the *Cornishman* on 7 June 1917. It included the following verses:

> Weep not; they would not have us weep for them;
> Weep not; for they are as the stars that shine;
> Their glory spilt upon the darkened skies
> Can not be dimmed by frailty, yours or mine …
> And above all the foam-girt shores that make
> This land our land, England their own, the Queen
> Of lands – aye, bid us not forget they fought
> To keep her name and honour always green.

Basil Granville has no known grave. He is remembered on the Arras Memorial and the Helston War Memorial in Cornwall.

Continue. The track bends round to the right ❾ but carry on for 200m and stop. You are now roughly on the spot where Second Lieutenant Alfred Oliver Pollard MC entered the German trenches during a reconnaissance on the night of 16 April 1917. Pollard had risen from private to second lieutenant in the HAC and had already been awarded the DCM for his part in a bombing duel in Sanctuary Wood near Ypres on 30 September 1915 – earning the nickname 'Bombo' – followed by the MC on 26 March 1917. As battalion bombing officer on 16 April Pollard led his men from Hill 80 then cut across country from the railway line further back down this track. Reaching the German wire the party cut through and entered the German trench here where they heard Germans talking in a dugout. German sentries were roused and after a helter-skelter escape Pollard found that two men were missing. Although he returned to find them, they were gone – probably picked up by a German patrol. For his actions here that night in carrying out 'a dangerous reconnaissance of the enemy's front line under very heavy fire' and obtaining 'most valuable information', Pollard was awarded a bar to his Military Cross on 18 June 1917. By then, however, he had already been awarded the **Victoria Cross** for performing another extraordinary feat of courage, attacking a German strongpoint near the line of the railway, just this side of the electricity station and less than 200m away in the field to your right. In fact not one but two VCs would be awarded for actions here.

190 Brigade had not succeeded in securing the flank along the railway as intended when Gavrelle had been captured on 23 April 1917. Nevertheless, a flank had been created – the new front line facing north and northeast and running from Hill 80 to the eastern outskirts of Gavrelle for almost 2km – but the village had become enclosed in a dangerous – tighter – salient. As the Germans had denied 4/Bedfords the high ground around the Windmill the pressure on Gavrelle remained and further attacks on Oppy and Arleux to the north could not be contemplated. This would mean further attacks by the RND a few days later.

Look into the fields to the south to a point in the heart of the group of pylons which was the site of a key German strongpoint on the left flank after the 23 April attack.

For the next major attack on 28 April 1917, 1st and 2nd Battalions, RMLI of 188 Brigade of the RND were selected. To the south of Gavrelle 2/Marine Battalion was to extend the salient with a company from **Anson Battalion** protecting its right flank. Meanwhile, 1/RMLI was to attack to the north of the village – astride the track here in the direction of the D33 Rue de Gavrelle up ahead – supporting the attack of the Canadian Corps and 2nd Division against the Arleux Loop trenches and Oppy. C Company – Second Lieutenant Reginald 'Bill' Haine – and D Company of 1/HAC were to support 1/Marine

The slight dip in the ground in front of the nearest pylon on the right marks the approximate position of the German strongpoint attacked by Reginald 'Bill' Haine and Alfred Oliver Pollard. (Courtesy of Paul Oldfield)

Battalion's assault by bombing north up the German trenches at right angles to the assault to capture the strongpoint near the railway and join hands with the 1/RMLI. 'The Boche were north of us and the dividing line between us was a light railway', recalled Haine, '... this was banked up and the Germans had a terrific strongpoint ... with several machine guns.' Both sides recognized the importance of this strongpoint as being the key to the outcome of the attack.

When the attack went in at 4.25am on 28 April 1917, the preliminary bombardment had failed to cut the German wire and the 1/RMLI attack against the Prussian Guard stalled immediately. Many men of 1/RMLI were shot down here – where you are standing – by machine-gun fire from the strongpoint on the railway line to your right. It had to be neutralized.

Second Lieutenant Haine's commanding officer, **Lieutenant Colonel Charles 'Ozzy' Osmond**, ordered Haine 'to do something about it'. Haine led three successive attempts to capture it but was driven back each time with heavy losses. It was almost 9.00am. Haine rallied his men for a fourth assault whilst D Company, which had bombed up the German support line under Captain O'Brien, gave covering fire from the rear. In a flurry of Mills bombs Haine carried the strongpoint capturing about fifty men and two machine guns and even going as far as 100m into the field to the left of the track here but it was too late for 1/RMLI, whose dead and wounded lay all around you.

When the inevitable counter-attack came at about 10.00am, Haine and the survivors of C Company held on for 2 hours but were eventually forced back south of the railway line and the Germans re-occupied the strong point.

For the rest of the day and throughout the night the Germans threw themselves against Haine's depleted force but they clung on.

A renewed attack by 4/Bedfords and 7/Royal Fusiliers was ordered for 4.00am on 29 April and Haine's CO met him and asked for a repeat performance of his attack on the strongpoint. 'You've got to do it again', he said. 'Good God', exclaimed Haine and asked if his friend Alfred Pollard's intact B Company could do the job instead, as they had been in reserve but Osmond replied, 'Bill, I dare not risk it'. Haine duly led another attack – his fifth – on the strongpoint and a wounded Prussian fleeing back along the trench created panic amongst the rest of the garrison holding the strongpoint. Around fifty Prussian Guard surrendered and by 7.15am the position was secured. Haine's Victoria Cross was assured. Now it was his friend's turn.

Alfred Pollard's B Company was fed in and they passed through Haine's exhausted band to hold the trench north of the strongpoint. Responding to a German counter-attack Pollard took two men – 1/HAC bombers **Lance Corporal Victor Scharlach** and **Private Reginald Hughesdon** – and began bombing and clearing the trench towards you.

Pollard told Hughesdon and Scharlach that he was going to move slowly up the trench; the firing of his pistol being the signal for them to throw their Mills bombs immediately, to land about 15m in front of him. This would pitch them in the next traverse – beyond their position. They only had two bombs each.

Setting off along the trench, they dodged around traverse after traverse, Pollard leading the way with his revolver. Soon they were 100m ahead of any other British troops but pressed on having been joined by **Lance Corporal John McCarthy** of 13/Royal Fusiliers. They covered another 100m or so without meeting any Germans. Pollard recalled:

> Then suddenly as I entered one end of a stretch of trench between two traverses, a big Hun entered the other, rifle and bayonet in his hand. I fired; he dropped and clapped both his hands to his stomach. Almost instantaneously with my shot I heard the whizz of Reggie's bomb as it passed over my head. A second man appeared behind the first; I fired again and he dropped like a stone. Bang! Bang! The two bombs thrown by my followers exploded one after the other. The third man saw the fate of his predecessors and turned to go back. Those behind, not knowing what had happened, tried to come forward. I fired again. Bang! Zunk! went the remaining bombs of our small store.

They even hurled back German stick bombs when they came flying over.

Pollard's small party fought like men possessed and cleared the trenches up to this track and beyond, to a point 450m off into the fields to your left according to official 188 Brigade reports. At this point, **Lieutenant Ernest Samuel** arrived with the rest of Pollard's B Company. Lewis gunners were placed in shell holes on either side of the trench facing north enabling troops of the 2nd Division to link up with them and so secure the front line. The second of 1/HAC's VCs in 24 hours had been well and truly earned. Between them Haine and Pollard's companies had managed to achieve what 1/RMLI – and before them 4/Bedfords and 7/Royal Fusiliers – had failed to do: secure the German front line north of the railway. For their part in the latter action Reg Hughesdon was awarded the DCM and Scharlach and McCarthy the MM.

Both Haine and Pollard survived the war. Haine received the MC for his actions in Afghanistan in 1919 and in 1956 became a founder member of the Victoria Cross/George Cross Association. Pollard – one of only two men who could boast the combination of DCM, MC and Bar and VC to their name for deeds during the First World War, the other being Australian **Captain Joe Maxwell** – went on to serve in the RAF in the inter-war period and authored over forty books, including a 'concise history' of the RAF in 1934.

Alfred 'Bombo' Pollard receiving his VC from King George V.

Continue to the junction with the D33 and stop. Oppy Wood is to your left but look right, down the road, towards the large electricity station. ❿ You will shortly be traversing the ground – from north to south – which was the scene of two attacks by the Pals battalions of the 31st Division on 3 May and 28 June: the first a failure, the second a success.

The 31st Division relieved the exhausted RND in the line on the night of 29/30 April 1917. It was committed almost immediately to another large-scale assault to advance the line north and south of Gavrelle – officially the Third Battle of the Scarpe – over unknown ground alongside the 2nd Division on 3 May. The by now infamous windmill and the spur on which it stood would be the fulcrum of the attack as it dominated the ground towards Oppy, threatened any attack from north or east and denied the Germans observation to the south. Captured at great cost on 28 April by 2/RMLI, it had been held by just forty Marines until relieved. Now the 31st Division had to hold it to secure its grip on Gavrelle and so ensure the success of this next phase of the Battle of Arras.

The line of what was known as **Bradford Trench** strikes the road at this point, which is apt as it was here, to either side of this junction, that 16/West Yorks – 1st Bradford Pals – assembled on the left flank of 93 Brigade to attack the German line which ran from Oppy Wood, crossed the D33 a little to your left then ran towards Gavrelle in the fields across the road. On their left were the Hull Pals of 92 Brigade attacking Oppy Wood whilst to their right – attacking across the road from behind the electricity station – were the 2nd Bradford Pals of 18/West Yorks up to the outskirts of Gavrelle near the windmill – note how the ground rises gently to the windmill spur just before the band of trees on the horizon. The Leeds Pals of 15/West Yorks were just beyond the spur, south of the Route Nationale: the present day D33E. These three battalions, recruited by two of Yorkshire's great industrial cities in 1914, had been severely mauled at Serre on 1 July 1916 – see our *A Visitor's Guide – The First Day of the Somme* – and were keen to do well.

Imagine now a bright moonlit night in the early hours of 3 May 1917 as the 1st and 2nd Bradford Pals began to assemble along taped lines in the fields here and to your right for the attack. German Very lights added to the illumination and there was no doubt that Pals were seen as heavy machine-gun and artillery fire opened up on them, killing and wounding many. Some of the Pals had to crawl over the dead bodies of their comrades to get into position. The British barrage opened at 3.44am and the attack went in a minute later.

By now the moon had set and the Bradford Pals went forward into the darkness of an early May morning compounded by a ground mist and the dust and smoke of exploding shells towards Oppy Wood to your left and the road to your right. They reached their first objective – the lightly held German outpost line – as did the Leeds Pals attacking Gavrelle Trench southeast of the village, but got no further. The effective destruction of the Hull Pals at Oppy Wood allowed the unhindered Germans to pour a heavy fire across these open fields from the direction of Oppy Wood and Oppy *Riegel* – **Link Trench** to the British – which ran west–east to the right of the road, some 450m or so to your left, and from clusters of machine guns on the windmill spur to your right. In addition, the Germans shelled their own outpost line.

Bradford Pal **John McGrath** 'trotted over' as an officer's runner. He remembers an officer urging the men forward with shouts of 'come on, come on!': 'I went about 70 yards then there was a cloud of dense smoke … I was hit: it took all my clothes off … blood was shooting out of my arm'. His officer told him to get back and McGrath never saw him again. It was all over by 8.30am: 'we are back in our old assembly trenches' noted the 31st Division diarist. Altogether the three West Yorkshire Pals battalions had suffered 274 officers and men killed – including many 'originals' with their '15', '16' and '18' regimental number prefixes – and hundreds more wounded and taken prisoner.

Turn right on to the D33 towards the electricity station. The road now begins to cut through the ground over which 18/West Yorks attacked – from right to left – on 3 May. This same road also bisected no-man's-land on 28 June 1917 when it was the scene of a limited but ultimately successful attack on **Cadorna Trench** – which ran roughly parallel to the road some 150m off in the field to your left – by a sister brigade of the 31st Division. On that day 94 Brigade – also badly beaten and bruised on 1 July 1916 – attacked with 13/York and Lancs (1st Barnsley Pals) and 11/East Lancs (Accrington Pals) to the north of the track you have just left, the Sheffield City Battalion (12/York and Lancs) here in the centre and 14/York and Lancs (2nd Barnsley Pals) on the right flank, assaulting the windmill spur ahead.

After 300m or so you will notice a metalled farm track coming in at right angles from the left. This track roughly marks the mid-point of the front allotted to the Sheffield City Battalion which attacked with three companies – D, C and A from north to south – from Railway Trench, which ran diagonally northwest–southeast through the present site of the electricity station. Unlike the 3 May attack, the men of the Sheffield City Battalion were moved up into their assembly positions almost two days before zero to deceive the Germans into thinking it was a routine relief but it was a long wait and German shelling added to both casualty figures and frayed nerves.

At 7.10pm the British guns hit Cadorna Trench with a blistering barrage, levelling it in places and smashing machine-gun posts and strongpoints as the leading waves of Sheffield City men swarmed out of Railway Trench and into no-man's-land, pausing only to straighten their lines along this road, where it becomes a little sunken further on. Hugging the barrage, they were through the German wire and into Cadorna Trench without a single casualty before the German artillery could retaliate.

Two of the first men into the German trenches and engaged in hand-to-hand fighting were a Barnsley colliery manager's son, **Second Lieutenant Frank Hellewell Westby**, and **Sergeant R.A. Jarvis** MM. Another leading his company's charge and playing a key role in the success of the assault was 33-year-old **Captain Vivian Sumner-Simpson**. Simpson, a Sheffield-born, married pre-war solicitor, had been a gifted amateur 'scratch' golfer and footballer for Sheffield Wednesday, scoring on his debut – aged 19 – against Manchester City in March 1902, and in several games of Wednesday's Division 1 title-winning season of 1902/03 and the FA Cup winning run of 1906/07. He was selected to be capped for the England amateur team to play Holland on Easter Monday 1907 but found that his 'other engagements' made it 'impossible for sufficient time to be spared for the journey to The Hague'. One of the first Kitchener volunteers to join the City Battalion as a private in 1914, he was awarded the Military Cross for his actions in the fields to your left for being 'the first man into the enemy trench ... involved in hand-to-hand combat with the defenders. Later he brilliantly organised the consolidation of the newly won position'. No less a figure than Field Marshal Sir Douglas Haig presented him with his medal on 16 July 1917.

To the north of the Sheffield City Battalion, 13/York and Lancs and 11/East Lancs had been equally successful, as had 14/York and Lancs against **Cairo Alley** further down the road towards the windmill spur. By the time the German artillery managed a reply the fighting was effectively over. It had taken just 7 minutes.

94 Brigade worked like fury to consolidate the newly won Cadorna Trench – named after Italian general Luigi Cadorna – the Sheffield City Battalion alone filling 7,000 sandbags in 6 hours to build up its new 250m-long front line in the field to your left under German shellfire and the teeming rain of a thunderstorm. In all, 94 Brigade took over 200 prisoners and counted almost 300 German dead on their sector and by the time it was relieved on the night of 30 June/ 1 July 1917 – almost a year to the day since it had suffered losses of 18 officers and 495 other ranks and had been all but destroyed – the Sheffield City Battalion recorded casualties of 8 killed. Total 94 Brigade casualties were 29 killed and 160 wounded. Cadorna Trench had at least served to lay some Somme ghosts.

The sportsman soldier Captain Vivian Sumner-Simpson was killed by a sniper in the village of Outtersteene on 13 April 1918 serving with 13/York and Lancs whilst 'moving amongst the men, cheering them up with his unquenchable optimism'. He is buried in Outtersteene Communal Cemetery Extension grave I.E.56.

Frank Westby was taken prisoner on 26 March 1918 also whilst serving with 13/York and Lancs and was repatriated in December that year.

Continue and after another 175m take the next track on the left marked

Captain Vivian Sumner-Simpson MC.

'no through road'. This is the old Oppy road that connected with the Impasse d'Oppy at the French 23rd Dragoons memorial before the dual carriageway was constructed. You are now ascending the windmill spur. The original road went straight ahead where it now bends to the left. The memorial to the French Dragoons is just across the dual carriageway.

Proceed around the bend and just before the electricity pylon on the left and the fork in the track, stop. The track was the old road to Izel lès Equerchin. The Gavrelle windmill ⓫ was some 50m or so in the fields to the left. By 1914 this was the site of the last of what had been three Gavrelle windmills and standing here one can appreciate its dominant position and why the armies of both sides wrestled so viciously to retain or gain control of the ground on which it stood.

After the Bavarians had occupied the mill and the spur here in the early morning of 2 October, the French counter-attack came into their right flank at 9.30am; not from the west – from the direction of the Point-du-Jour – but from a line between Oppy and Neuvireuil to the north. It was in the fields here that Sous Lieutenant René Grabias-Bagnéris led a dismounted attack on the windmill with ten of his dragoons and an infantryman and died in a hail of fire from a German machine gun positioned at one of its windows. After the first counter-attack had been repulsed the fighting lasted all day and it was not until 5.00pm that the line stabilized here. By nightfall 1st Battalion Bavarian RIR 12 was bivouacking in and around Gavrelle; houses burned in all corners of the village. By midnight the battalion's field kitchen moved in and the village became congested with men and materiel. The church was immediately pressed into use as *Verbandsplatz* (dressing station) under a large Red Cross flag but, according to German accounts, was 'heavily shelled by the enemy nevertheless, killing many wounded men'.

The windmill was held by the Germans until around 7.00am on 28 April 1917 when 5 Platoon of B Company, 2/RMLI under **Lieutenant George Arthur Newling** captured it during a fierce struggle. Forty Marines managed to hold on to this vital position and outposts around it against thirteen counter-attacks until two guides led in two platoons of 15/West Yorks during the night of 29/30 April 1917. George Newling was awarded the Military Cross in July 1917 for his 'conspicuous gallantry in an attack', when he led his platoon with great courage and skill, and held the objective, when captured, against numerous counter-attacks. Newling survived the war and had six children, one of whom, Michael, flew Hurricanes during the

Battle of Britain, ejected over occupied Belgium and escaped in May 1940 and was awarded the Distinguished Flying Cross in February 1941. Flight Lieutenant Newling went missing on 6 July 1941 whilst flying a Spitfire with 111 Squadron.

There was heavy fighting for the windmill again during the ill-fated Pals attack of 3 May 1917. The failure of the attack by 18/West Yorks and the Leeds Pals, who were unable to get beyond their first objective – Gavrelle Trench – south of the Route Nationale, exposed the windmill position. Defended by four Vickers guns of 93 Company Machine Gun Corps (MGC) and two trench mortars in a shell crater by the ruined mill, shellfire destroyed two machine guns facing east and killed the crews and the mortar ammunition ran out. Two men buried the mortars whilst **Second Lieutenant Hugh Smyth Piggott** of 18/West Yorks took charge and tried to organize a defence:

> I saw the enemy advancing slowly from shell hole to shell hole about 50 yards away. They were bayoneting the wounded … 2 guns … were out of action so I ordered Sergeant Richmond and a man to fetch the 2 guns from B Trench. They dashed over the bullet swept open and Sergeant Richmond brought his gun back. The enemy were bombing B Trench severely.

Despite a fierce struggle the Germans pressed their advantage home and Smyth Piggott's position became untenable at about 7.25am:

> The last machine gun being out of action, and as the enemy were on both flanks and in front, I ordered the withdrawal and sent Sergeant Cranley … and Sergeant Richmond to cover our withdrawal with rapid fire … This was effective and we got away … all the time … these two sergeants continued sniping and accounted for about 15 to 20 … they thus saved our being outflanked from the windmill.

The Germans came on and recaptured the windmill. **Sergeant Nathaniel Cranley** (40) of 93 Company Machine Gun Corps was killed trying to save his comrades. He has no known grave and is remembered on the Arras Memorial.

Now it was the turn of C Company of 18/Durham Light Infantry (18/DLI) – the Durham Pals – under sergeant turned **Second Lieutenant Harold Everett Hitchin** DSO, MM and Bar to be thrown into the see-saw struggle for the windmill.

Retrace your route to the bend and stop. Turn right to look into the field. It was across this very ground that the men of Harold Hitchin's C Company launched their attack to recapture the windmill on 3 May 1917.

News had come in that the windmill had been lost at 5.30am and Hitchin was ordered to retake it. His past exploits proved he was the man for the job. Hitchin had enlisted in 12/DLI as a private in 1915 and by 3 May 1917 had proved his mettle. In 1916 he had been awarded a MM and Bar before being commissioned and posted to 18/DLI. In March 1917 he and **James Bradford** – brother of Roland Boys Bradford VC – had rushed and bombed German positions near Gommecourt, for which exploit he had received the DSO.

Hitchin led his company up **Foxy Alley** to a point where the communication trench became shallow and he could get no further – somewhere around the dual carriageway overpass, about 100m west of the present location of the 23rd Dragoons Memorial. After a hurried and inconclusive reconnaissance, during which he noted there was 'no cover whatever' and saw no Germans, he decided on a frontal attack with three platoons in two waves. At 6.45am he ordered his men in under **Second Lieutenant Lean** and immediately German SOS rockets were fired from shell holes west of the windmill bringing shrapnel raining onto no-man's-land. C Company reached the area of the dual carriageway slip road behind you unmolested but as they charged across this ground towards the railway line just 30m or so into the field here they were hit by 'a hail of machine-gun fire' from the line of the railway and from the south, across the dual carriageway. Lean's platoons were driven back to the area around the Dragoons' Memorial. Now Hitchin took command and led his men forward again to within 45m of the windmill where he paused before the final assault. At that point the Germans began to retire under the attentions of the British artillery. The resulting barrage also hit Hitchin's force – reducing it by 50 per cent – and again he was forced back to the road. Hitchin now decided on a slow methodical advance 'by small fighting patrols'. Imagine now the remainder of Hitchin's force crawling – snake like, in small parties – from shell hole to shell hole across this ground, one man moving forward whilst the others laid down covering fire, edging ever closer to the windmill. By 11.30am Hitchin had forced the Germans back and had cleared them from the house to the south of the windmill with rifle grenades. The ruined windmill was once again in British hands and Hitchin went on to recover 4 Vickers guns and 2 Stokes mortars before C Company was relieved by 13/York and Lancs on the night of 4/5 May. For his leadership in recapturing the windmill position Harold Hitchin was awarded the MC. He was badly wounded in June 1918 but survived and served as a major in the Second World War with 15/ and 14/DLI in the United Kingdom. Harold Hitchin devoted his time to bee-keeping after his retirement and died in Wales in 1975.

Although the windmill had been recaptured there was a high price to pay. The area around the ruins here now resembled a charnel house and was remembered with loathing by those who had to hold it.

D Company of the Sheffield City Battalion was sent up to hold the line here on 9 May 1917 and **Private Donald Cameron** remembered that the windmill was 'a horrible place. You dared not move or show yourself during the day … It was the worst place I had ever been in … There were bodies and bits of bodies all over the place; British and German. A butcher's shop. It stank to high heaven'.

Casualties were heavy. By the time the Sheffielders were relieved on 14 May 1 officer and 5 men had been killed and 3 officers and 63 men had been wounded or gassed. **Private T.C. Hunter** kept a diary and his single word entry for each of the days 9 to 13 May are identical: 'hell', 'hell', 'hell', 'hell' and 'hell'.

Four days later 11 Platoon of C Company, under 39-year-old **Second Lieutenant Charles Pimm**, was back at the windmill and was shelled mercilessly. Lieutenant Frank Westby, following up, stumbled across a 'slaughter house' with **Sergeant Joseph Gould** – a pre-war teacher – standing in the centre of it: 'Where is your platoon, sergeant?' asked Westby, 'All dead except three of us', replied Gould. With Pimm dead Sergeant Gould had assumed command, dug several of the men out with his bare hands and put them under cover. Gould was later commissioned but was killed on 13 October 1918 serving with 1/5 York and Lancs.

Before you move on imagine now the assault on the senses as you survey the scene here and recall the words of **Richard Sparling**, who served in, and wrote the history of the Sheffield City Battalion:

the dead around the windmill seemed numberless … there were bodies in all stages of decomposition. All were either grinning black or ghastly blue. The stench was awful. Once when digging … men came across something round. The men hit it, and it wobbled. They dug a bit further and it was found to be a dead German, with arms folded. He had been killed in his 'cubby hole'. They covered him up with a groundsheet and sandbagged him in.

There is little doubt that many men still lie beneath these now peaceful fields.

Continue and turn left to take the metalled track which goes downhill for 30m – banks to either side – to meet the D33. Turn left, under the dual carriageway, passing the Impasse d'Oppy on the left to reach the staggered crossroads. Turn left on to the D33.

You are now following the route taken by **Commander Arthur Asquith** as he led a party of men from the Hood Battalion to capture the last bastion of German resistance around the mayor's house during the final phase of the battle on 23 April 1917. Continue for some 150m until you reach the hotel Le Manoir de Gavrelle and turn right into the car park. The rather grand house to the right of the drive was rebuilt in 1922 on the site of what was the mayor's house. This – the last house on the south side of the Gavrelle–Fresnes road – was the furthest extent of the advance of the Hood Battalion under their commanding officer Arthur Asquith that day. Asquith – the third son of the ex-prime minister Herbert Asquith – was up in the front line with his men at this stage of the attack and on emerging into the open from the village found that the attack was held up by fire from a trench, roughly 200m to the east of this car park, several machine guns about 700m east of Gavrelle cemetery and others around the windmill. Asquith had identified a determined knot of German resistance centred here, on the mayor's house, as the key to the final capture of the village. This trench – which became the new German front line – Gavrelle Trench – could not be attacked until the threat of the mayor's house had been nullified.

Asquith had first attempted to attack up a ditch from the south – from behind the rear garden of the mayor's house – but his party had been beaten back with losses in officers and men. He had to find another way. Returning to the crossroads you have just left, Asquith gathered up a party of men and raced down the road, bursting into the mayor's house and taking ten prisoners in a short struggle. Asquith recalled that, incredibly, given the noise and fury of battle, several Germans were found to be 'sleeping or shamming sleep' in the two cellars! Snipers were posted upstairs facing east along with a Lewis gun and other snipers in other rooms of the house and Asquith handed its defence over to **Sub Lieutenant Cooke**. Cooke took a Lewis gun out into the open to harass the trench but was repulsed with heavy loss so Asquith knew that he would get no further before dark so decided to consolidate what he held and ordered the men of Hood and Nelson to dig in. At 7.23am, he finished scribbling a message to his brigadier, **Lewis 'Chico' Philips**: '7.12am Gavrelle taken'. It was Asquith's 34th birthday, St George's Day and the second anniversary of the death of one of his great friends from the early days of the Hood Battalion, the poet **Rupert Brooke**. Despite this it did not stop the British 'heavies', uncertain of the situation, dropping 'shell after shell into the buildings of the mayor's house' from about 11.00am, forcing some defenders into the cellars and others to retire.

Return to the road and look east. During the afternoon of 23 April a remarkable scene unfolded just down the road here which Asquith later reported on: 'An enemy car drove up to within 150 yards of the mayor's house, was Lewis gunned by us [and] turned round revealing a red "X", picked up an officer from trench [east] of mayor's house, and drove back to Fresnes'.

Turn left and retrace your route to the staggered crossroads then turn left on to Rue de Plouvain. In a little over 200m you will see a lane on your left immediately after house No. 18. This lane follows the exact line of a ditch along which Arthur Asquith moved to try and outflank the German garrison in the mayor's house and Gavrelle Trench. He reported that his group ' pushed up the ditch . . . in hopes of outflanking this enemy trench'. They got to a point about 200m along the ditch which was 'very shallow and at one point it [was] necessary to jump out over a metre gauge railway, under strong sniping at close range'. Asquith recalled that he saw the helmets of between twenty to thirty Germans in the trench and then 'four of us went up the ditch. Lieutenant [Charles] Asbury [commanding A Company] and one of the 2 men were shot dead. It became evident that the heads of enemy occupants of this trench must be kept down if the trench were to be attacked by a flanking rush. I therefore went up the street towards the mayor's house'.

Asquith retraced his steps and came out of the ditch here before heading up the Rue de Plouvain to attack the mayor's house. It was only when he had returned from his successful mission there that he was told a single shell had killed another two of his company commanders – **Lieutenants James Morrison** (C Company) and **Gerald Hornby Tamplin** (D Company) – at this very spot.

Continue downhill to find **Gavrelle Communal Cemetery** ⑫ on the left. Stop. Gerald Tamplin's body was originally buried, along with several men of Howe Battalion, both known and unknown, in a small battlefield cemetery on ground which is now behind the houses directly opposite the cemetery gates. His identity disc was intact when his remains were exhumed after the war and he lies today in **Point-du-Jour Military Cemetery** (III.G.14). Lieutenant

James William Morrison has no known grave and is remembered on the Arras Memorial.

It was north to south along the road here that Arthur Asquith ordered his Hood Battalion to dig in on 23 April 1917, connecting ditches and shell holes to fashion a new front line joining with that of **Drake Battalion** a little further down the road to the south.

Enter the cemetery and look towards the back wall. Asquith placed a Lewis gun and some riflemen along the eastern boundary as an outpost protecting the new front line. It is also worth noting that this is roughly the mid-point of the front on the start line held by 15/West Yorks – Leeds Pals – when they attacked Gavrelle Trench on 3 May 1917.

The attack started at 3.45am and the Pals reached the German outpost line. **Private Arthur Dalby** went over just to the south of here and remembered that it was:

> easy … to get into the German trenches … because the Germans had emptied [them] and put their artillery on them within a yard or two … They let us get across and they had vacated their trenches and … when we got in them they blew them to hell. They blew us as well. Seven of us came back out of 27 in my section.

Machine guns missed by the leading waves enfiladed the captured ground from right and left and the following waves faltered. The commanding officer, **Lieutenant Colonel Stuart Campbell Taylor**, knew his battalion's momentum had evaporated and watched in horror from his headquarters, somewhere just across the road from the cemetery gate, as a group of about a dozen German prisoners being shepherded back towards him suddenly turned on their captors, seized their rifles and took them prisoner. Taylor feared a counter-attack would break his line and organized a line of resistance but despite at least three attempts to attack the position the Germans were held off by a combination of reinforcements from 18/West Yorks, 12/King's Own Yorkshire Light Infantry and artillery fire. As in the northern sector the attack here failed with heavy losses and the Leeds Pals suffered grievously; 10 officers and 164 other ranks were killed and 2 officers and at least 27 men were taken prisoner with scores more wounded. Lieutenant Colonel Taylor was awarded the DSO on 18 July 1917 for saving a 'critical situation'.

Gavrelle Communal Cemetery

Enter the cemetery. You will see a distinctive black and grey granite memorial stone directly in front of you. Inaugurated on 8 May 1995 – the fiftieth anniversary of the end of the Second World War in Europe – this commemorates **Abbé Pierre Carpentier** who was born on 2 July 1912 at Libercourt, 25km north of Gavrelle but brought up in the village. Ordained into the priesthood on 29 June 1938, he still had to fulfil his military obligations and attended the St Cyr military academy, leaving with the rank of sous lieutenant. Called up when war broke out in September 1939, he was demobilized in October 1940 after the German subjugation of France. Returning to the priesthood he took up a position as abbé of the parish of St Gilles in Abbeville and became involved in the Resistance movement, helping to smuggle Allied airmen out of France and into Spain. Betrayed by British-born petty criminal, con artist, army deserter and Gestapo informant Harold 'Paul' Cole in Abbeville on 8 December 1941, Carpentier was beheaded at Lubeckerstrasse jail in Dortmund with nine others on 30 June 1943.

Behind the memorial are two small CWGC plots containing the graves of seven British soldiers – infantrymen and Royal artillery anti-tank gunners – who were killed during the 1940 France and Flanders campaign, the majority of whom were involved in the defence of Arras and the surrounding area in May that year.

Leave the cemetery and turn left. A few metres beyond the communal cemetery – on the site of the raised ground beyond the southern cemetery wall – was a large, well-tended German cemetery, complete with large memorial. Begun in 1915, after the German occupation, it gradually grew to almost twice the width of the village cemetery. At the time of writing – May 2017 – the land here was being developed as a small housing estate.

Continue. The road bends left and gradually becomes lower than the ground to either side. This section was known as the 'Sunken Road' and it was here – digging in along a line 40m out into the field to the left and parallel to the road – that the advance of Drake Battalion under **Commander Walter Sterndale-Bennett** DSO came to a halt on 23 April. Drake attacked on the right flank of 189 Brigade's front, mainly south of the village and so did not have to engage in house-to-house fighting like the Nelson and Hood Battalions. Sterndale-Bennett – aged 23 at Gavrelle and an inspirational leader – was one of the youngest men to command an 'infantry' battalion during the First World War. He had helped to get his men through the thick German wire at the start of the 23 April attack – D Company suffering heavily – and into the German trenches. The Drake then advanced to the line of the Rue de Roeux – the 'yellow line' – across the field to your right, and after reorganizing pushed on over the open ground towards the road here. Now imagine the scene at this spot at around 6.00am on 23 April as you read Walter Sterndale-Bennett's account of the action:

> The advance continued and wherever the enemy showed fight, our men made immediate dashes at him and put him out of action or (in a few cases) sent him back as prisoners. The men's blood was up and few prisoners were taken. Owing to our having suffered pretty badly in the enemy's wire the men had little mercy. In the SUNKEN ROAD there was a considerable enemy garrison. They started to bolt but about 400 of them were reorganised under an officer and at one period it looked rather as if they were going to hold up the [13/King's Royal Rifle Corps to the right] … Our advanced parties were ordered to rush up to the SUNKEN ROAD and attack the garrison on their right flank. They did this in excellent style bringing up a Lewis gun and enfilading the road. Those of the enemy that were left gave themselves up and had to run the gauntlet through our men as they ran back to the rear. The same Lewis gun took up a position on the eastern side of the road and played on the remainder of the garrison which was doubling towards SQUARE WOOD … When the remainder of the [battalion] came up we immediately pushed out our Lewis guns on to the high ground to the east of the road and gave our men a short rest. During this period many more of the enemy were cleared out of the small shelters in the SUNKEN ROAD and enemy tools were being collected. I then went out to site my trenches … Keeping the men as much as possible off the road, they started to dig in.

As the road rises gently you will see a road on the right. This was the right flank of the Drake Battalion, where it was in touch with 13/KRRC. Sterndale-Bennett had his men dig north from here towards a small party of RND digging in just north of the cemetery. This trench became the British front line until 28 March 1918 and was named **Willie Trench**. **Towy Post** was later established on this ground and Towy Alley Communication Trench ran back from it. Sterndale-Bennett – grandson of the composer William Sterndale-Bennett – was awarded a bar to his DSO for his leadership at Gavrelle. A shell severed one of his legs below the knee and shattered the other foot on 4 November 1917 near Passchendaele and he died three days later at Dozinghem.

Turn hard right at the junction. **Invicta Trench** ran east cutting across the angle of the road here, whilst **Towy Alley** ran to the right. The Germans had launched their attack on the British Fifth Army on the Somme on 21 March 1918 and on the 23rd a 'land mine' exploded under the British wire of Towy Post. The garrison of **Gavrelle Post** north of the cemetery disappeared two days later. The portents were ominous. The German juggernaut eventually hit the British line held by B Company 16/Londons under **Captain George Arthur Norman Lowndes** at Towy Post – on the ground in the triangle formed by the sunken road and this one – at about 7.05am on 28 March 1918, after a 2-hour bombardment. Captain Lowndes remembered what happened:

> Up went the SOS from Gavrelle Post … up went three SOS signals on our right. 'Here they come sir!' rang out from the dugout sentry. Up went the Towy SOS. On the instant the sentry had dived down the dugout steps to get the men up. For a few seconds … perhaps the longest seconds of my life – I stood on the fire step watching alone … Quite suddenly the smoke cleared; and there, barely 200yards in front, were the enemy in full view bearing down on us in a compact huddled mass … as the smoke lifted … I counted five lines each … five deep. So deep in fact that I had to rub my eyes to make sure that they were not new belts of wire grown up in the night! … Out of the dugout poured the thirty or forty survivors of B Company. In an instant the rattle of rapid fire, a fire sustained almost continuously for an hour till rifles were red hot and bolts jammed, broke out from every fire bay around the cross formed by the junction of 'Towy' and 'Little Willie'.

With the garrisons of all but one of the other advanced posts north of Gavrelle virtually wiped out, the Germans broke into Willie Trench, outflanked Towy Post and began to bomb up Towy Alley from behind. Gavrelle had already fallen and the Westminsters fought like demons, many were killed:

> By 7.45am we were completely surrounded … strong enemy bombing parties were working down Invicta to the right and Towy trench in front … The end came suddenly … stick grenades began to fall thickly, three or four at a time around us

… Reluctantly I gave the order, 'Withdraw slowly … fighting down Towy.'

Lance Corporal Lionel Samuel and his signallers stayed with their power buzzers to maintain communications and remained after Towy Post had fallen. The Germans rushed over the open cheering wildly trying to finish the job and Captain Lowndes saw his 'greatest school friend' take action: 'It was Innes Stitt, poet, dreamer, Scholar of Balliol, who stopped them! That was the last time I was with him … a short figure, silhouetted in my mind forever against the growing dawn, up on the parapet revolver in hand covering the withdrawal.'

Continue and at the next junction turn right onto the **Rue de Roeux**. Towy Alley cut across the road at right angles 25m or so further on. The remnants of Captain Lowndes' command passed this way on their fighting withdrawal back to Naval Trench, 700m away beyond the houses on the left. Official documents state that only Captain Lowndes, **Second Lieutenants L.W. Friend** and **John Prince** and 25 men made it back through the German bombers to Naval Trench, although Lowndes himself recorded only 2 officers and 17 men escaping out of a garrison of nearly 110. Joining the garrison of Naval Trench they 'put up a spirited resistance' against German infantry advancing 'continuously in lines of men shoulder to shoulder' before resuming their dogged fighting withdrawal, 'contesting every yard of ground' to the area of Ditch Post you visited earlier. Captain Lowndes was awarded the Military Cross for his leadership that day. He went on to become an educationist and author of several books. **Innes d'Auvergne Stewart Stitt** (aged 19), the Marlborough educated son of the Revd and Mrs Mary Stitt of Stretham Rectory, Ely, Cambridgeshire, was never seen again. He is remembered on a memorial tablet in St James's Church, Stretham and the Arras Memorial. Stitt had co-authored a short book of poetry – *To-morrow and Other Poems* – in 1917, a verse from which is inscribed on the Stretham memorial and became his epitaph: 'Think not that we made fine sacrifice, heroic with sacrificial sighs: But moved to an end appointed meet, and the incomplete that we made complete'. Lionel Samuel, from Wembley in Middlesex, was captured and imprisoned in Parchim prisoner-of-war camp, Mecklenburg.

Second Lieutenant Innes d'Auvergne Stewart Stitt.

After 400m you will see Rue de Fampoux on the left. You now have a choice of either continuing the route to visit **Naval Trench Cemetery** or visiting the cemetery after you have returned to your vehicle. To visit the cemetery turn left along **Rue de Fampoux** and continue until you reach a fork with a green CWGC sign. Bear right along the farm track and after 450m you will see a grass track on the right leading to the cemetery. ⓭ The junction of Towy Alley and Naval Trench was at this junction of tracks.

Naval Trench Cemetery
Naval Trench Cemetery stands on the line of what was the German front line of 23 April 1917 and was named Naval Trench by the RND which had converted it into its second line by the summer of 1917. By late March 1918 Naval Trench had become the British second line of resistance and was occupied by the headquarters of **Lieutenant Colonel 'Phil' Mannock Glasier** DSO of the Queen's Westminster Rifles on 28 March. Here the Westminsters held the Germans at bay until the British artillery blew down a block at the junction of Towy Alley and the Germans 'swarmed into the Naval Line, surrounded and either captured or killed the remainder of the garrison between Gavrelle road and the south'.

Naval Trench was retaken by 6/Black Watch on 26 August 1918. Thirty-five men from the RND are buried here, all killed or wounded

Naval Trench Cemetery.

during July, August and September 1917. Whilst there are no graves resulting from the attack on Gavrelle on 23 April, five of the casualties are the result of a successful trench raid carried out on 7 September 1917. One of these men was 19-year-old **Able Seaman Ernest Barlow** (B.3) serving with the Anson Battalion, who is buried next to 21-year-old **Able Seaman John Bickerton** (B.2), both boys hailed from County Durham. The only officer buried here is 23-year-old **Lieutenant Austin Cook** (D.9) of 2/RMLI, whose name is on the St David's College War Memorial, Lampeter. Gazetted in June 1915, his name also appears on the St Mary's Church Memorial, Haverfordwest. There is one member of the 31st Division here, 21-year-old **Private Walter Titford** (D.10) from Warminster was killed on 14 May 1917 serving with 11/East Yorkshires. A former errand boy, Walter was one of four children and enlisted in August 1914. There is a single burial from 1940; 32-year-old **Captain Robert Miller** (C.1.A) was commanding D Company, 2/Cameronians (Scottish Rifles) when he was killed on 21 May at Gavrelle.

Retrace your route to the road, turn left and then left again at the junction on to the D33. Continue, passing the church on the right, to the junction with the main road and turn left onto the D33E – the Route Nationale. After 70m you will reach the *Mairie* on the left where there is a plaque on the wall to the right of the main entrance commemorating the men of The Queen's Westminster Rifles who

The plaque to the Queen's Westminster Rifles at the Gavrelle Mairie.

fought here on 28 March 1918. After the war Gavrelle was 'adopted' by Westminster Council, the adoptions fostered by an organization named the British League of Help, launched in the summer of 1920 by Lilias, Countess Bathurst, to 'seek out for each war devastated town and village in France a British "god-parent" community to give it practical aid and sympathy in its reconstruction'.

Continue, over the mini-roundabout, to find the 63rd (Royal Naval) Division Memorial on the right. **⑭** Take extra care here as vehicles often exit the dual carriageway at speed a few metres further on. Sited on the German front-line position of 23 April 1917, the memorial is the result of the efforts of a small group of dedicated individuals to mark the RND's remarkable achievement in capturing Gavrelle that day with a tangible monument. Designed by RND historian **Trevor Tasker**, its centrepiece is a 3-ton nineteenth-century anchor – the symbol of the RND – dragged up from Milford Haven and donated by Her Majesty's Salvage and Mooring Depot at Pembroke Dock. The huge anchor is surrounded by what look like shattered walls and broken brickwork, representing the ruins of Gavrelle and the RND's fight through the built-up area. Badges of the 63rd RND's units are mounted on the locally sourced brickwork and battlefield debris from the surrounding fields is a feature of the design. Built in

The Royal Naval Division Memorial.

1990, it was dedicated on 5 May 1991. Looking out across the open fields to the south you will see the Cross of Sacrifice of Naval Trench Cemetery visited earlier.

This road was the boundary between 189 and 190 Brigades, Nelson Battalion attacking here with The Hood following up. Commander Arthur Asquith – in the centre of his leading wave – jumped the gun and followed The Nelson 10 minutes into the attack to avoid his men being shelled. He arrived here in the German front-line system – the 'blue line' – at about 5.00am, reorganized and sent back twenty prisoners. Now came the hard part: fighting through the buildings of Gavrelle.

Turn and retrace your route back down the D33E3 towards your vehicle in the village centre. You are now following in the footsteps of the men of the Nelson and Hood Battalions as they began their bitterly contested advance towards their next objective – the road running south to Roeux – fighting house to house and cellar by cellar all the way. Asquith recalled that:

We advanced again slowly and half right through the village … The enemy were still sniping at our men from cottages. They were fired at by our men and rushed, and a good deal of mixed fighting at 20 yards range took place … a few of our guns were still firing short and were causing casualties among our men.

Leading Seaman Joe Murray was with The Hood:

fighting in a village is different from fighting in the open … Jerries were in the cellars and we were in the open and by then it was quite light so we were perfect targets … there were bricks flying about, rifle and machine gun fire. You couldn't keep any formation. Sometimes you got under a half blown-down house and other times you got over the top … however, you could not climb over the 10 to 15 feet of bricks that had formed.

Murray came across a badly wounded sub lieutenant and turned him over: 'there was a sort of grin on his face, which was red because of the brick dust, as well as the blood. Because of the smoke and dust you had to spit all the time … and you also kept rubbing your eyes'.

Continue and after the *Mairie* pause at the crossroads marking the junction of the D33 signposted Roeux and Fampoux. In 1917 the road ahead, which passes the church, did not exist. This spot was the crossroads of the road to Roeux to the right and the old road to

Izel lès Equerchin. That road led to the old windmill and after the war – until the dual carriageway arrived – it would have passed the monument to the 23rd Dragoons.

Turn right to follow the original advance of the Nelson and Hood Battalions. The line of this road was the second objective – the 'yellow line' – on 23 April 1917. It was here that Commander Asquith paused to reorganize for the next phase of the operation at 5.40am. Your journey from the RND Memorial took mere minutes but it took Asquith 40 minutes of hard fighting to reach this spot: 'at the yellow line we reorganised. The street was crowded with Nelsons and Hoods in addition to about 100 Bedfords ... who should have been north of the main Arras–Fresenes road [you have just left] defending our left flank. I collected their three officers and asked to move north of the road.' Asquith had to wait 20 minutes on this road for the British barrage to move on which he thought was a 'great mistake, giving the enemy a breathing space just when we have them on the run'.

Take the next turn left into the **Rue de l'Église** and as you head east imagine the noise, dust, smoke and smell of the British barrage, crashing down amongst the roofs of houses and cottages followed by the men of the RND, still fighting to winkle out the Germans from their protective cellars. From here they fought through, eventually breaking out into open country where they were halted by determined resistance from the mayor's house and the German trench to the east.

The church on your left was destroyed, this one dates from 1926. It was used by the Germans as a field hospital on the day they occupied Gavrelle on 2 October 1914 until April 1917. Inside the church is a wooden cross – **The Hood Cross** – complete with names taken from a contemporary casualty list. It was commissioned and paid for by Arthur Asquith, who was proud of his battalion's part in taking and holding Gavrelle in spite of repeated counter-attacks.

By the time it was relieved by the 31st Division at the end of April 1917 the fighting for Gavrelle had cost the RND more than 3,000 casualties.

As you pass the church to return to your vehicle, glance at the eastern wall. It suffered shell impact damage during the Second World War but this has been repaired. The eagle-eyed will, however, still be able to make out where the damage was.

Note the impressive village war memorial – inaugurated on 29 May 1917 – on which are inscribed the names of seventeen soldiers and two civilians of the village. One of the civilians – **Victorine**

Capron – was killed during the British preliminary bombardment prior to 23 April 1917. A further nine names record the dead of the Second World War. The northern face bears a memorial to the French 34th Division whilst the eastern face features another memorial to the 23rd Regiment of Dragoons, which fought up near the windmill on 2 October 1914. The bas-relief on the western face portrays St Germaine, the patron saint of Toulouse, marking that town's sponsorship of Gavrelle and its assistance in rebuilding the village after the war.

If you wish to break for refreshment before moving on, a visit to Chez Bernadette (previously called Café des Sports) will also allow you to view a copper plaque to the 31st Division, one of two items hand-made by Gavrelle veteran **Joe Yarwood**, who served as an RAMC stretcher bearer with 94/Field Ambulance in the 31st Division. He later recalled his time on this sector:

I had the wind up good and proper when I was at Gavrelle. We came out … looking like people out of Belsen, what with the strain of that 10 days – our eyes were sunk in the back of our heads because we'd been through the mill good and proper. It was the roughest passage I ever had frankly.'

In 1990 Joe read the story in a local paper about the huge anchor being transported to Gavrelle for the RND Memorial and decided to make a memorial offertory plate for the church:

The cafe at the crossroads is now called Chez Bernadette.

As I had a hobby – copperwork – I said I'd be happy to make them a plate that they could flog towards their funds. On the plate were three panels: the 31st Division – my division – ... the Royal Naval Division [and] the third panel had Vimy and then round the centre ... it had got Gavrelle 1917. About 14 inches across; all worked by hand. They said after inspecting it they weren't going to sell it ... but take it out to Gavrelle when they opened the memorial ... It was dedicated by a local clergymen.

Route 6
Arras Central

A tour beginning at: Place des Héros

Coordinates: 50°17′27.89″ N – 2°46′38.55″ E
Suitable for: ♦ ♿ 🚗
Maps: Série Bleue 2406E – Arras

General description and context: Arras is an ancient city. The capital of the Artois region of northern France, its prosperity in the Middle Ages had been based on the trade in wool and fine tapestries. Before the war the two main squares – the Grande Place and the Place des Héros or the Petite Place – had been the beating heart of Arras, their fine facades betraying the city's historic past as a prized possession of the rulers of the Austro-Spanish Netherlands.

Occupied by the Germans briefly in September 1914 the French had quickly cleared them from the city but had not driven them too far. By the time the lines of trenches had solidified over the winter of 1914–15 Arras found itself in a salient jutting out to the southeast. Surrounded by the Germans, who were never more than a mile or two beyond the ancient centre, Arras was also overlooked from the German positions on the high ground of the Vimy Ridge to the north. And so began the long agony of Arras at the hands of the German gunners.

By February 1916 the damage to many of the city's architectural gems, including the cathedral and its two beautiful main squares, was all too evident. German shells regularly sought out the unwary at important road junctions and the railway station and sidings.

Private Harry Drinkwater arrived in Arras in early March, 1916 with 15/Royal Warwicks and he witnessed the desolation:

This morning I had a look round Arras. It's an awful show; imagine a town like Bath or Leamington burnt out and you have Arras. Going along one thoroughfare I saw a huge hole in the ground – was told it was here a 'Jack Johnson' had dropped. A 'Jack Johnson' is a huge shell fired by the heaviest

The Hôtel de Ville *in Place des Héros.*

of the German long-range guns. It was named Jack Johnson after the black boxer of that name who had been very much to the fore in the boxing world in the days immediately before the war and because of the havoc caused on its explosion. On this occasion it had gone right through the ground and exploded in a subterranean passage. It had made an awful mess ... There are still one or two shops open ... They keep their goods down the cellars where they stay themselves and we bartered through the grating and paid through the nose.

To move large numbers of men around on the surface in daylight was hazardous in the extreme but below ground a veritable warren of ancient subterranean quarries – *Les Boves* – had been dug out of the chalk along with connecting passageways, shelters and storage silos. There was enough space in these and in the vaults beneath the cathedral precinct and the Bishop's Palace to shelter entire divisions and that is exactly the use to which they were put by the British when they finally took responsibility for the defence of the city from the French.

The ruins of the Hôtel de Ville *after German shellfire destroyed it in 1915.*

This is not so much a route around Arras that begins and ends in a specific place, but more a guide to some of the First and Second World War sites that can be visited today. Consequently, we have not provided a map as a very good street plan of the city can be obtained from the Tourist Office, where details of the free local Citadine bus service and the Arras City Pass, can be obtained. Alternatively, Arras can be navigated successfully by bike and there are a number of dedicated bike routes within the city. Visitors should be aware that market days do impact on parking in central Arras and are as follows: Place des Héros: every Wednesday and all day on Saturday; Grand Place and Place de la Vacquerie all day on Saturday.

Directions to start: We suggest the tour of the city begins at Place des Héros where the Tourist Office is located on the ground floor of the magnificent *Hôtel de Ville*. Their address, should you wish to contact them beforehand, is: Hôtel de Ville, Place des Héros, 62000 Arras, or email: contact@explorearras.com.

The Église Saint Jean Baptist on Rue de la Housse.

Église Saint Jean Baptist

A short walk from the Place des Héros is **Rue de la Housse** which leads you to **Place de Ipswich** and the imposing **Église Saint Jean Baptist**. Ipswich is twinned with Arras and has had a long affiliation with Arras stemming from both world wars but not least from the aid provided in the immediate aftermath of the First World War.

With the city and its surrounding agricultural infrastructure utterly devastated, residents of Ipswich and the county of Suffolk were in the vanguard of the efforts to revive farming in the area freely providing advice and practical help in the form of machinery and seed for new crops to help the people of Arras rescue their agricultural economy.

To the right of the church entrance portal is a plaque commemorating the bravery of **Warrant Officer Wacquez** and **Augustus Glasson**, two firefighters who were killed during the fire that 'ravaged' the church in 1915. Inside the church there are several artefacts which make a visit worthwhile and, apart from the Rubens painting depicting the descent of Christ from the cross, the altar and altar piece – both in marble – date from the seventeenth century and were part of the original chapel in the Petite Place – now Place des Héros – which was destroyed in 1792.

The Arras Tunnels

Much of Arras was built using stone excavated from quarries beneath the city, these excavations left huge underground 'pillar and stall' cavities, *Les Boves*. As early as 1914 the French garrison in Arras located the medieval chalk caverns that lay beneath the brewery and sawmill on the Bapaume road, and used them as deep shelters to protect troops from the German artillery bombardments. Yet, it was only towards the end of 1916 that the tunnels under the city's eastern suburbs were occupied with a view to continuing the mine warfare that so characterized this sector of the front. In October 1916 the 350-strong **New Zealand Tunnelling Company** carried out a topographical survey and quickly came to the conclusion that the existing network of underground workings could be comprehensively developed and used in a large-scale offensive.

By 8 April 1917 these tunnels had developed into an extensive network capable of sheltering over 24,000 men, of whom 13,000 could be sheltered in the town square sector alone. **Alan Thomas**, a company commander serving with 6/Royal West Kents, 12th Division, remembered them in April 1917 as being a safe haven from enemy shelling:

> The caves (for there were a series of them) were filled with every modern convenience: electric light, running water, braziers for cooking, a miniature railway and even furniture, though this consisted mostly of empty crates and petrol cans. Here, in these caves, we lived for over a week. No sound reached us from the

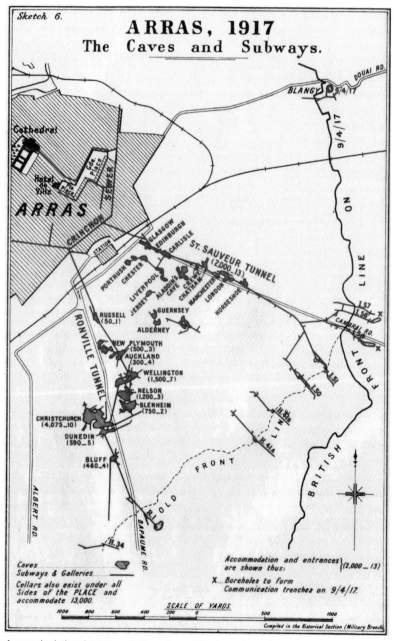

Sketch 6.

ARRAS, 1917
The Caves and Subways.

A map depicting the two main branches of the Arras tunnels.

A. Waiting Ward For Iceland Dressing Room cases.

B. Reserve stretchers.

C. Iceland Dressing Room.

D. Hunter Waiting Ward.

E. Medical Quarter Masters Strs.

F. R.A.M.C.Officiers Quarters.

G. Quarters For R.A.M.C. personnel.

H. Hunter Dressing Room .

J. Operating Theatre (Surgical Specialist).

K. Cookhouse.

L. Quarters For Reserve Or Resting Bearers.

M. Mortuary.

N. Officiers Ward.

O. Dynamo Water Stand Pipe.

P. Exit Lobby.

⊔⊔ Deep Trench Latrines.

Passages And Spaces. Unmarked Were User AS Wards

0   10   50   100

Scale of Feet

Entrance from Iceland St

N

Entrance From Hunter St

Well fitted Cottage pump

Exit to Rue St Quentin

A plan of Thompson's Cave, a casualty clearing station which was established under Rue St-Quentin in February 1917.

outer world. Very occasionally a small chip of chalk would drop from the roof, sign that a heavy shell had landed overhead.

The network was composed of two main arteries, the first, which ran under the road to Cambrai, was called the **St Sauveur** tunnels and was largely allocated to the 9th and 34th divisions prior to the

'The Iron Door' in Rue de Saumon.

opening of the Battle of Arras on 9 April 1917. Here the influence of the British sappers can be found with the chambers named Crewe, Carlisle, Glasgow, Liverpool and Chester. One of the main entrances to the St Sauveur tunnel complex is located in **Rue du Saumon** through what was called 'The Iron Door', a portal that still exists today. The second network was the **Ronville** branch, which ran almost parallel with the D917 to Bapaume and whose chambers were christened by the New Zealanders with names exclusively from their homeland, hence: Auckland, Wellington and Christchurch. This system became home to units of the 3rd, 12th and 29th divisions and could house some 9,000 men, whilst the smaller St Sauveur tunnels could accommodate over 2,000. At the end of the two tunnel systems the New Zealanders drove narrow saps out into no-man's-land under the thick belts of barbed wire, saving countless lives leading up to and during the final moments before zero hour in April 1917.

Wellington Quarry Museum
Situated on **Rue Arthur Delétoille**, the quarry is part of the Ronville system and was opened in March 2008. The museum consists of a visitor's centre displaying historic artefacts and presenting the

The entrance to Wellington Quarry Museum.

historical context of the Battle of Arras. The tunnels are accessed via a lift shaft that takes visitors approximately 20m below ground to the galleries. Visitors are taken on a guided tour which lasts about an hour through some 350m of tunnels to see audio-visual presentations of various aspects of the campaign and the soldiers who built, lived and worked in them. At various places, graffiti and painted signs can be seen, along with relics left by the troops. Keep an eye out for the **Hampshire Cross** which was carved by **Private Harry Bowring** sometime after 15 April 1917. Bowring was serving with 2/Hampshires and had just returned from the battalion's costly attack on Infantry Hill, east of Monchy-le-Preux. There is free parking and the quarry is open all year round from 10.00am to 6.00pm with an hour's break for lunch beginning at 12.30pm. Full price at the time of writing was €6.90 with the concessionary rate being €3.20. Tickets can also be purchased online from the website or alternatively, at the Tourist Office – http://www.explorearras.com/fr/visiter/carriere-wellington.

Within a few minutes walking distance south along the Avenue Fernand Lobbedez – the D917 – is the **Memorial to the New Zealand Tunnelling Company**, which was inaugurated in April 2007 and is situated at the intersection of the D917 and Rue Alexandre Ribot.

Les Boves Beneath the Grand Place and Place de Héros

The medieval sewers and cellars beneath the Grand and Petite Places were linked to the Crichton sewer and were one of the first areas to be connected by the New Zealand Tunnellers. First dug in the tenth century, a guided tour reveals an extensive system running beneath Arras which was used by the wealthy merchants who owned and lived in the magnificent gabled houses around the city's impressive squares. Running short of space in their own homes they stored their goods below ground. Today, the underground car park in the Grand Place owes its existence to these medieval cavities. Access is via the Tourist Office from where tickets can be bought and the times of the tours can be confirmed. At the time of writing the price of admission for adults was €5.30 and €3.10 for children and over 65s.

Palais St Vaast and the Cathedral

This enormous building is situated behind the *Hôtel de Ville*. From the top of the narrow **Rue Désiré Bras** you can see the great buttresses of the Cathedral, **Notre-Dame de l'Assomption et St Vaast**, complete with a profusion of impact marks from the bombing raids of the Second World War. The Palais was the BEF's GHQ in 1940.

The southeastern end of Arras Cathedral with the buildings of Palais St Vaast to the left.

Walk down the street, turning right at the bottom to find the entrance to the Cathedral on your left. The original building was begun in 1778 but was only completed after the French Revolution. Sadly, it was almost completely destroyed during the First World War and only opened again in 1934. Harry Drinkwater remembered a 'canteen rigged up by army chaplains from which we ... buy coffee and biscuits' in the Cathedral's vaults. Harry called it the 'Soldiers Rest'.

Arras survived the Second World War, suffering just bomb damage in 1944. As you walk round the building you will notice the plaque to **Victor-Jean Perrin** (1894–1971) who was appointed Bishop of Arras in 1945. Perrin fought as a lieutenant in the First World War before being ordained in 1921. He enlisted again in 1940 and fought the Germans at Rennes. On the same column can be seen the memorial tablet to the British and Empire dead of the First World War; similar to those found in cathedrals across northern France. Leave the Cathedral by the same entrance you used to enter the building, retrace your route past Rue Désiré Bras and follow the railings to the junction with **Rue Paul Doumer**. You are now walking alongside the Palais St Vaast, which you can see on your right. At the end of the street, turn right to find the imposing entrance gates to the **Palais St Vaast** courtyard. Today, it is the entrance to the **Museum of Fine Arts**, which occupies a large section of the Palais St Vaast and is well worth a visit. Opening times and entrance costs can be obtained from the Tourist Office but it is worth remembering that entrance is free on the first Sunday of the month and on European Heritage days. After you leave the Palais St Vaast turn right to reach the entrance to the **Jardin de la Légion d'Honneur**. Just after you pass through the gates you will find two memorials on the left. The first is the Royal Tank Regiment Memorial and the second is the Welsh Guards Memorial. Both of these memorials relate to the 1940 battles for the city.

Faubourg d'Amiens
The Faubourg d'Amiens Cemetery, the Arras Flying Services Memorial and the Arras Memorial are to be found on **Boulevard du Général de Gaulle** and can be accessed by the local Citadine bus service which tours the city. If you are using your own vehicle there is parking in the lay-by next to the cemetery, the car park opposite or further along the boulevard where there are parking areas.

The British and Commonwealth section of the cemetery was begun in March 1916, and continued to be used by field ambulances and fighting units until November 1918. The cemetery was enlarged

The British cemetery at Faubourg d'Amiens and the Arras Flying Services Memorial.

after the Armistice when graves were brought in from the battlefields and from two smaller cemeteries in the vicinity. Today, the cemetery contains over 2,650 burials of the First World War, 10 of which are unidentified. The graves in the French military cemetery were removed after the war to other burial grounds and the land they had occupied was used for the construction of the Arras Memorial and

Arras Flying Services Memorial. This is another cemetery where the sheer number of headstones is almost overwhelming: the impact being magnified when one considers that each headstone tells its own story and marks the last resting place of a young man who died for his country. Amongst the myriad headstones here is that of 20-year-old **Private Philip Jinks** (I.C.39) of 15/Royal Warwicks, the best friend of diarist Private Harry Drinkwater, who stayed with him until he died during the German attack near Roclincourt on 4 June 1916. Also here lies **Captain Arthur Colthurst** (I.H.14) of 15/Gloucesters who was killed in action on 25 October 1916. His youngest son, 33-year-old **Flying Officer John Colthurst**, was killed whilst serving as a bomb aimer with 115 Squadron on 24 February 1944. John's body was never recovered and is now commemorated on the Runnymede Memorial. His second son, 42-year-old **Commander Anthony Colthurst** RN was killed whilst in command of HMS *Avenger* in November 1942 when she was sunk by U-155. Only twelve of the crew survived. His name is commemorated on the Lee-on-Solent Memorial. Arthur's wife, Maria Colthurst, never remarried and died in 1949 of a broken heart. If you have a few minutes to spare, plant your cross of remembrance by Arthur Colhurst's headstone and contemplate the sacrifice that his family – and many others like it – made in both world wars.

The adjacent **Arras Memorial** commemorates almost 35,000 Commonwealth casualties who died in the Arras sector between the spring of 1916 and 7 August 1918 – the eve of the Advance to Victory – and have no known grave. The most conspicuous events of this period were the Arras offensive of April–May 1917 and the German attack in the spring of 1918. There are thirteen recipients of the Victoria Cross commemorated here and amongst them six who won their awards in the Arras area (**see Appendix 1**). In Bays 8 and 10 you will find the names of two brothers, 29-year-old **Rifleman John Standcumbe**, serving with 9/Londons, 56th Division, who was killed near Héninel and 19-year-old **Private Samuel Standcumbe**, of 15/DLI, 21st Division, who was killed near Henin Hill. Both boys lost their lives on 10 April 1917.

The **Arras Flying Services Memorial** commemorates some 1,000 airmen of the RFC, the RNAS and the RAF who were killed on the Western Front and who have no known grave. The memorial contains some very well-known names, **Major 'Mick' Mannock**, **Lieutenant Arthur Rhys-Davids** and **Captain Douglas Bell**, to mention but three.

The Mur des Fusillés, depicting the replaced execution post and the plaques commemorating the names of the executed French Resistance fighters.

Mur des Fusillés

This site can be accessed via Avenue du Mémorial des Fusillés, which leads through the Bois de Citadele to the site – **Mur des Fusillés** – where the German garrison executed French resistance prisoners during the Second World War. Civilian opposition to the German occupation of the Arras region was relentless and 218 of the resistance fighters were executed in the ditch of the Vauban fortress. After you pass through the metal gates and turn the corner, the execution post and the names of the dead, which are on the surrounding walls, make this an altogether sombre spot.

The Citadel

The entrance to the Citadel is 250m further down the Boulevard du Général de Gaulle and can be accessed by walking across the bridge which spans the moat. The Citadel was built according to plans drawn up by French military engineer **Sébastien le Prestre de Vauban** between 1668 and 1672 on the orders of Louis XIV (1661–1715). The aim of the Citadel was to protect the city from attack but it was rapidly nicknamed 'the beautiful useless' because of its position, which was hardly strategic! The Citadel houses the oldest chapel in the city: the Chapel Saint Louis, dating from the seventeenth century

The entrance to the Citadel.

and, from April to October, the **Salle des Familles** hosts an exhibition presenting the history of the Citadel. Up until July 2009 the Citadel was home to the 601st Infantry Regiment but after is disbandment the Citadel was sold to Arras for what had been described as 'a token sum'. Entrance is free, apart from certain restrictions from mid-June to mid-July (details from the Tourist Office). Tank enthusiasts will be interested to know that during the build-up to the April 1917 offensive, tanks were kept hidden from enemy view in the ditches surrounding the Citadel, camouflaged beneath netting and it was from here that Lieutenant Weber's *Lusitania* departed on its way to **Railway Triangle** on 9 April 1917.

37 Brigade Advanced Headquarters
Number 1 Rue du Temple stands near the corner at the far northeastern end of the street. Given that Brigadier General Albemarle Bertie Cator and his 37 Brigade staff occupied this house over 100 years ago, it is remarkable that this fine red-brick building is still intact. The house was no more than 500m from the British front line which crossed the modern day D939 west of Tilloy-lès-Mofflaines. **Captain Alan Thomas** recalled the trenches were lined with bricks from local buildings: 'Your footsteps could be easily heard as you

37 Brigade advanced headquarters on Rue du Temple.

walked along them. So could those of the German sentries as they paced along their trenches, which in this small section of the line were no more than ten or fifteen yards away from ours.'

Graffiti on the external walls demonstrates that 37 Brigade was not the only unit to use the building. In March 1916 it was occupied by 1/DCLI and at the time of writing the black painted '1st DCLI' sign is still visible to the right of the large window, itself to the right of the front door. It appears that the house was also used as a barbers and the area around the doorway is covered with graffiti left by soldiers presumably waiting for a haircut. These include a variety of names, regiments, addresses and army numbers of men who unintentionally left a lasting memorial.

Post-war Arras

By the end of the First World War, Arras was in ruins. For almost three years, from October 1914 to April 1917, the various garrisons had lived largely below ground under the almost continual shelling of the German artillery, an experience that Alan Thomas described as 'an amazing blend of civilization and desolation'. By the end of the war only 5 per cent of the houses in the city were habitable; **Palais St Vaast**, together with much of the remaining architectural heritage in the city, was completely destroyed. After the Armistice, the French government decided that faithful reproductions of these ancient buildings should be built in their original locations as a tribute to the city's medieval heritage. Thus, the chief architect responsible for France's national monuments, **Pierre Paquet** (1875–1959), was given the formidable task of rebuilding Arras from a mass of rubble. Using photographs and archive documents, Paquet designed facades faithful to the spirit of the original buildings whilst ensuring the interiors were built to modern specifications. Apart from the main monuments and historical buildings, the city was largely rebuilt in the art deco style, which is most visible on many of the house facades along Rue Gambetta, Rue Ernestale and **Place du Théâtre**, where the guillotine was an almost permanent feature during the French Revolution.

Appendix I

Where to Find the Victoria Cross Winners

Between 21 May 1916 and 26 December 1918 thirty-two men were awarded the Victoria Cross for gallantry in the field in the region covered by this guide and its companion volume *The Battles of Arras – South: Bullecourt, Monchy-le-Preux and the Valley of the Scarpe*. Of these, five were won on 9 April, the opening day of the Battle of Arras. Thirteen awards were made posthumously and the recipients are buried or commemorated within the Arras area.

Name	Date of Death	Where	Reference
Jones, Lieutenant Richard *8/Loyal North Lancs*	21 May 1916	Broadmarsh Crater	Arras Memorial, Bay 7
Milne, Private William *16/Battalion CEF*	9 April 1917	Vimy Ridge	Vimy Memorial
Sifton, Lance Sergeant Ellis *18/Battalion CEF*	9 April 1917	Vimy Ridge	Lichfield Crater Panel 2, Column 2
Pattison, Private George *50/Battalion CEF*	10 April 1917	Vimy Ridge	La Chaudière Mil Cemetery (VI.C.14)
Waller, Private Horace *10/KOYLI*	10 April 1917	South of Héninel	Cojeul British Cemetery (C.55)
Mackintosh, Lieutenant Donald *2/Seaforth Highlanders*	11 April 1917	Fampoux	Brown's Copse Cemetery (II.C.49)
Cunningham, Corporal John *2/Leinsters*	12 April 1917	Bois en Hache	Barlin Communal Cemetery (I.A.39)

Name	Date of Death	Where	Reference
Hirsch, Captain David *4/Yorkshires*	23 April 1917	Wancourt	Arras Memorial, Bay 5
Harrison, Second Lieutenant John *11/East Yorkshires*	3 May 1917	Oppy	Arras Memorial, Bay 5
Jarratt, Corporal George *8/Royal Fusiliers*	3 May 1917	Pelves	Arras Memorial, Bay 3
White, Sergeant Albert *2/South Wales Borderers*	19 May 1917	Monchy-le-Preux	Arras Memorial, Bay 6
Cassidy, Second Lieutenant Bernard *2/Lancashire Fusiliers*	28 March 1918	St-Laurent-Blangy	Arras Memorial, Bay 5
Kaeble, Corporal Joseph *22/Battalion CEF*	8/9 June 1918	Neuville Vitasse	Wanquetin Com Cemetery (II.A.8)
West, Lieutenant Colonel Richard *Tank Corps*	21 August and 2 September 1918	Croisilles	Mory Abbey Military Cemetery (III.G.4)

Appendix 2

Writers, Poets and Artists Killed at Arras

Men such as Isaac Rosenberg and Edward Thomas need little introduction and were well known in their respective circles before the war. Others, such as Arthur West – who rose to prominence after the publication of *The Night Patrol* – and Robert Beckh – whose work was published posthumously in *Swallows in Storm and Sunlight* – were killed before their writing became established. Sadly, many more of the men in the list below who lie either in the region covered by this guide or its companion volume – *The Battles of Arras – South: Bullecourt, Monchy le Preux and the Valley of the Scarpe* – fall under the heading of forgotten poets and writers of the First World War.

Date of Death	Name	Designation	Reference
30 April 1916	Pitt, Second Lieutenant Bernard *10/Border Regiment*	Poet	Arras Memorial, Bay 6
15 August 1916	Beckh, Second Lieutenant Robert *12/East Yorkshires*	Poet	Cabaret Rouge British (Marquillies Comm. Cem. German Ext. Memorial 24)
3 April 1917	West, Captain Arthur *6/Ox & Bucks LI*	Poet/Writer	HAC Cemetery (VIII.C.14)
9 April 1917	Thomas, Second Lieutenant Edward *Royal Garrison Artillery*	Poet	Agny Military (C.43)
9 April 1917	Scanlan, Lieutenant William *5/Battalion CEF*	Poet	Barlin Communal Cem Ext. (I.H.75)

Date of Death	Name	Designation	Reference
9 April 1917	Wilkinson, Second Lieutenant Walter *1/8 Argyll & Sutherland Highlanders*	Poet	Highland Cemetery, Roclincourt (II.A.5)
10 April 1917	Littlejohn, CSM William *1/7 Middlesex*	Poet	Wancourt British (V.E.16)
20 April 1917	Flower, Driver Clifford *Royal Field Artillery*	Poet	Arras Memorial, Bay 1
23 April 1917	Crombie, Captain John *4/Gordon Highlanders*	Poet	Duisans British (IV.A.22)
2 July 1917	Masefield, Captain Charles *1/5 North Staffords*	Poet/Writer	Cabaret Rouge British (VI.H.23)
23 March 1918	Wilson, Captain Theodore *10/Sherwood Foresters*	Poet/Writer	Arras Memorial, Bay 10
25 March 1918	Blackall, Lieutenant Colonel Charles *4/South Staffords*	Poet/Artist	Arras Memorial, Bay 2
1 April 1918	Rosenberg, Private Isaac *1/King's Own*	Poet/Artist	Bailleul Road East (V.C.12)

FURTHER READING

There are many published titles covering aspects of the Battles of Arras and limited space dictates that they cannot all be covered here. Five of the **Battleground Europe** titles published by **Pen & Sword** – www.pen-and-sword.co.uk – focus on the area covered by this guidebook and provide a host of supplementary information on some of the most visited parts of the area. Here you will find personal experiences of soldiers who served, contemporary photographs and trench maps.

Gavrelle, Kyle Tallett and Trevor Tasker
Oppy Wood, David Bilton
The Battle for Vimy Ridge, Jack Sheldon and Nigel Cave
Vimy Ridge, Nigel Cave
Walking Arras, Paul Reed

For battlefield visitors who wish to expand their knowledge with more in-depth reading, the following will be of interest:

Arras, Peter Barton and Jeremy Banning, Constable (2010)
Shock Troops: Canadians Fighting the Great War 1917–1918, Vol. 2, Tim Cook, Viking Canada (2008)
Harry's War – The Great War Diary of Harry Drinkwater, Jon Cooksey and David Griffiths (eds), Ebury (2013)
Into Battle, John Glubb, Cassel (1978)
Grandfather's Adventures in the Great War 1914–1918, Cecil Moorhouse Slack, Stockwell (1977)
Cheerful Sacrifice, Jonathan Nicholls, Leo Cooper (1999)
VCs on the Western Front – 1917 to Third Ypres, Paul Oldfield, Pen & Sword (2017)
The Underground War: Vimy Ridge to Arras, Philip Robinson and Nigel Cave, Pen & Sword (2011)
A Life Apart, Alan Thomas, Gollancz (1968)

INDEX